# Tell Me a Story I Don't Know

*Conversations with Chicago Sports Legends*

## George Ofman

### TRIUMPH
**B O O K S**

Library of Congress Cataloging-in-Publication Data

Names: Ofman, George, author.
Title: Tell me a story I don't know: conversations with Chicago
    sports legends / George Ofman; Foreword by Mike Greenberg.
Description: Chicago, Illinois: Triumph Books, [2023]
Identifiers: LCCN 2023029211 | ISBN 9781637275429 (paperback)
Subjects: LCSH: Sports stories—Illinois—Chicago—History. |
    Professional athletes—Illinois—Chicago—History. | Mass media
    and sports—Illinois—Chicago—History. | Sports—Illinois—
    Chicago—History. | Sports—Illinois—Chicago—Miscellanea.
    | BISAC: SPORTS & RECREATION / General | SPORTS &
    RECREATION / Football
Classification: LCC GV191 .O36 2023 | DDC 796.09773/11—dc23/
    eng/20230711
LC record available at https://lccn.loc.gov/2023029211

This book is available in quantity at special discounts for your group or organization. For further information, contact:

**Triumph Books LLC**
814 North Franklin Street
Chicago, Illinois 60610
(312) 337-0747
www.triumphbooks.com

Printed in U.S.A.
ISBN: 978-1-63727-542-9
Editorial production and design by Alex Lubertozzi
Photographs courtesy of the author unless otherwise indicated

*To everyone who contributed to helping make
my podcast a success and, eventually, this book*

# Contents

# *Foreword*

THAT DAY started out like so many thousands that have come since—I woke up, got my act together, and went to work. But that day was different from any of the rest that followed because it was the first, and anything you do for the first time is fresh and exciting; it hasn't had time to become dreary and mundane yet. It was also a Saturday, by the way, which was appropriate, in that the career path I had chosen was the furthest thing possible from a traditional nine-to-five.

I rode the El train directly into the Merchandise Mart. The stations were inside that iconic building on the Chicago River—both of them, the train station as well as the radio station, WMAQ All-News 67. My first day on my first job as a news production assistant consisted of shadowing, and assisting, the sports anchor who would be handling the afternoon sports updates, twice every hour amid the classic "you give us 22 minutes, we'll give you the world" format. I tiptoed into a tiny, crowded newsroom, the air thick with cigarette smoke, hopelessly overdressed in a suit and tie. As I recall, no one else was wearing so much as a collared shirt. (It was a hot, Chicago summer Saturday afternoon, and this was a radio station—if you know, you know.)

I was introduced to the sportscaster, and my first observation was that he looked a little like my hero, Groucho Marx. Then he began to talk, and I quickly realized he sounded like Groucho too. I would eventually find out Groucho was *his* favorite as well, but that came much later. We didn't talk about that the first day. What I do remember is that, when the sportscaster shook my hand, the news director said, "George, Mike here is going to be watching you today."

And George said, "Sounds good, I like to work with an audience." And so, on my very first day ever in the professional world, two months after I had graduated from college, George Ofman started teaching me how to be a sportscaster. The date was August 26, 1989. As it turned out, he would continue teaching me every single day for the entirety of the seven years I worked in Chicago.

George taught me how to write a sportscast. He taught me how to file a live report from a ballgame—be that from Wrigley Field, Soldier Field, or the blessed old Chicago Stadium, may it rest in peace. George was a pro's pro, then and now. His command of one of the nation's busiest and most passionate sports markets is second to none. It never ceased to amaze me, but it was 100 percent true: George knew everyone in town, and everyone knew George.

One other way in which George changed the trajectory of my life came in 1992, a few months after he and I had both been part of the launch of The Score (WSCR-AM), the first all-sports radio station in Chicago, and one of the first in the United States. I was a producer, behind the scenes, and George was the roving reporter, covering every game in town for the fledgling format found at 820 on the AM dial. About five months into what was still then an experiment, it was decided that George needed to be in the building most of the time to anchor the sports updates, for which he ultimately became a legend in the city. However, that left a gaping hole in the station's roster, and a big question: who would cover the games? It was George, along with one of the hosts, Tom Shaer, who stepped forward and said, "I think this Greenberg kid could do it." Two weeks later, I was in Cleveland with Michael Jordan and the Bulls for the Eastern Conference Finals. I was 24 years old, and my life would never be the same again.

All these years later, George has finally done what he should have done long ago, which is share all these stories he has accumulated from all these people he knows, most of whom wouldn't tell them to practically anyone else. His podcast is the most intimate, delightful stroll down memory lane any sports fan could ever take, and this book will allow you to take it along with him, anytime you want. Thanks for everything, George. And, as Groucho himself said, "Outside of a dog, a book is man's best friend. Inside of a dog, it's too dark to read."

—Mike Greenberg

# *Preface*

AFTER NEARLY 50 years in the sports broadcast industry, I decided to become an author. I'm not writing about the breadth of my career or one particular story. No, it's about my podcast, something that was an inspiration thanks to a fellow broadcaster. When COVID hit, WBBM Newsradio decided to put me on their hit list. I was let go in July 2020 as part of a cost-cutting move. Just two weeks later, something else hit me: the idea of doing a podcast. I had done so many interviews with players, coaches, management, etc., that simply doing something longform wouldn't be a problem. And it didn't take me very long to get going.

It was early August 2020 when, just a few weeks after I was let go by WBBM, I decided to explore doing a podcast. My idea was to interview top sports personalities and their connections to Chicago. It would not only entail a look into their professional lives but, in many cases, their personal lives, as well. And it was Laurence Holmes's interview of me on his podcast, *The House of L,* that was the springboard to *Tell Me a Story I Don't Know.*

Finding a job in radio now for what I do for a living is about as likely as finding a dinosaur roaming the Kennedy Expressway. Come to think of it, I *was* the dinosaur, the oldest sports anchor in town in a profession that had been dying for years. What was an industry that flourished from the late 1970s was diminishing due to a number of factors, including the Internet, cellphones, and a radio industry itself suffering a painful decline. So here I was, not even close to calling it a career, at a crossroads I didn't expect to meet this early.

The idea of venturing into the world of podcasting started with phone calls and emails, lots of them to people in the industry I knew and some I didn't. I must have touched base with two dozen folks, some who produced podcasts and others who hosted them. And then there was a plethora of how-to videos. I watched them all and listened to enough advice that I actually started talking to my wine bottles. Worse yet: they were talking back to me! Anyhow, I began the process by coming up with a theme and a name for the podcast. Since by then I had made many contacts during my 47-year career in the industry, I started thinking about some big names, such as Bob Costas, Mike Greenberg, Michael Wilbon, Marv Albert, and many others. I knew them all and had worked with most of them in some capacity.

With the name settled, I needed some theme music, so I scoured the Internet for free music. It was a long and exhausting process, finding the right piece of music—something upbeat but not over-whelming—but ultimately a successful one.

So I had the title and theme but, boy, did I still have a long way to go. Who would help me get started with a platform company that would serve my needs? Who would come up with the graph-ics? Who would help me mix while I did the interviews and edited them? And could I monetize it? It was now October, and I wanted to begin the podcast in November! I reached out to Dan Levy, a rather hulking guy with a booming voice. I had known him as he struggled through the radio industry but had now become a jack of all trades and a pretty damn good one at all of them.

"Dan, got anyone who could help me with the mixing?" I asked.

"Yes," he said and offered me a young protégé from Indiana named Will Hatczel, who was just getting his feet wet in the radio business.

I hired him and asked whether he knew a graphics artist. He said yes and offered me Tatiana Shinkan, better known as "TT." I got in touch with her and described what I was looking for. Within days she came up with exactly what I wanted. It was perfect and so was my caricature. Actually, it looked better than me in real life!

So now I had the theme, title, music, mixer, and graphics, but where was the podcast going? I talked to several platforms such as Podbean, Spreaker, and Anchor. While this was taking place, I reached out to a very dear friend, Dave Woloshin, the longtime voice of Memphis radio and the Memphis Tigers football and basketball teams. Dave and I have known each other since sophomore year in high school (Mather, on the North Side of Chicago). He was also part of my staff at WSIU Radio & TV. Days later, I received a call from a fellow named T.J. Rives. He is the sideline reporter for the Tampa Bay Buccaneers radio broadcasts, among several jobs he's held. T.J. told me Dave called him, and what he said afterward cemented a new relationship. "Any friend of Dave's is a friend of mine, and anything I can do to help you along the way I'll gladly do."

Wow! How lucky can you get? T.J. got us hooked up with RedCircle, a free platform. Then I went into action beginning the interview process while also accumulating a long list of guests and devising a concept of how I wanted the podcast to be laid out. I wanted to have at least a half dozen interviews in the can and ready to go before we debuted. The podcasts would drop on a weekly basis, and I figured since the Chicago Bears played most of their games on Sunday and with so much sports talk about them on Mondays, I would drop them on Tuesdays (except when the Bears played a Monday night game, then the podcast would drop on a Wednesday). We also devised a short preview, which we do run on Mondays.

I interviewed a number of guests prior to the podcast's debut. They included Bob Costas, Michael Wilbon, Mike Greenberg, Mark Giangreco, and Eddie Olczyk.

So now I had just about everything. The theme, title, music, mixer, graphics, platform, and guests. All I needed now was some sponsorship and a start date, and it wasn't going to be November and surely not December. I managed to convince the owner of the renowned Paulina Market on Chicago's North Side, Bill Begale, to invest in the program. I also managed to corral Vienna Beef Inc., home of the "Chicago hot dog" and an institution since 1893. Thanks to Keith Smith, the vice president of marketing, they joined us.

Now, the start date: January 12, 2021. But this turned out to be a possible issue if the Bears made the playoffs, so I decided to move it forward a week, to the 19th. This became a bigger issue. It was the day before the inauguration of Joe Biden as president of the United States, but the tumult surrounding the insurrection at the Capitol made this date way too questionable. That led me to the 26th, which happened to be the 35th anniversary of Super Bowl XX, when the Bears destroyed New England to win their first and thus far only Super Bowl.

Prior to our debut, I contacted several radio and TV writers in the city, asking if they would provide me with some publicity. They gladly did, from the now retired Robert Feder to the then *Chicago Tribune*'s Phil Rosenthal to current *Chicago Sun-Times* sports radio and TV writer Jeff Agrest. They were wonderful in giving me the platform I needed to get going, along with Fox 32's Lou Canellis and WCIU's Kenny McReynolds, both of whom had me on their TV shows. (Both, by the way, were guests on the podcast and are featured in this book.)

It was time to debut my new career: podcaster! We opened with much fanfare. Michael Wilbon was our first guest and a natural since he was born on the South Side of Chicago and still has a residence near downtown. Many, many more joined the parade.

We've been going ever since.

# BASEBALL

# Joe Maddon

IT WAS a century in the making. Actually, 108 years, to be precise. The Chicago Cubs won a World Series, and it took a bold front office, lots of talent, and an offbeat manager to tie it together. The insightful, creative, and at times quirky Joe Maddon harnessed the talent, and while it took a gut-wrenching seven games to finally get to the mountaintop, he delivered what many believed was impossible to generations upon generations of starving Cubs fans.

A title!

Wrigleyville was awash in unrequited joy. Relatives visited gravesites, where loved ones who rooted for the Cubs were granted a heavenly wish. A rousing parade and rally ensued. No more "wait until next year." Next year finally arrived.

But as the old saying goes, managers are hired to be fired. Only in this case, Maddon's contract was not extended after five years. What was a triumphant introduction at the Cubby Bear lounge, located across the street from the venerable Wrigley Field, turned out to be a sour ending, replete with finger-pointing and such. A disconsolate yet forward-looking Maddon left the Friendly Confines for his roots, the Anaheim Angels and a managerial post that turned into a disaster. In his third season, Maddon's Angels lost a dozen consecutive games, and he was shown the door. But it swung open to new venture, a book titled *The Book of Joe: Trying Not to Suck at Baseball and Life.*

Maddon's long journey to history began at age 27, when he was named a minor league manager. But he beat the bushes for some 25 years before he finally got a big-league managing job with the then Tampa Bay Devil Rays. Three years after taking over the moribund franchise, the Rays won 97 games and earned a trip to the World Series. Maddon was named Manager of the Year three times and used some unorthodox ways to motivate his teams, whether with slogans, bringing in pets to the ballpark, or letting his team dress up for road trips in onesies! The players bought in.

An extremely popular manager, particularly with the media, Maddon managed to turn skeptics into believers. But his book also ruffled feathers with some in the game, as he criticized the hand that fed him, analytics.

I was at the Cubby Bear the day Joe was introduced. It was a surreal experience, considering a loophole in his contract at Tampa Bay allowed Theo Epstein and Jed Hoyer to swoop in and make him the manager. Joe was excited, reflective, and funny. The audience in attendance was truly pumped.

As he approaches 70 (his birthday is in February), Joe would like to manage again, but the book may have scared off would-be suitors. He understands that. He also understands his role in transforming a franchise known more for its ballpark than success into a champion.

"It was exhilarating to become manager of the Cubs," he said. "I remember flying into the city, and we're landing at O'Hare and looking at all those houses as you're flying over the tops of them, and you're going to be attempting to influence a lot of people here. I felt confident, though I can't tell you why. But I always felt good about my methods and how I do things."

Those methods included the myriad slogans he used, such as, "Try Not to Suck," "Embrace the Target," "Everybody In," and "Own It Now." The last one he used for the 2019 season.

"Theo told me the press conference would be at the Cubby Bear, which I had no idea what the Cubby Bear was. And then you get there, and I look out the window as I sit in front, and I can see my name on the marquee at Wrigley Field. Wow! So you're sitting there, addressing everybody and what you believe in and how you're going to get this done. And you're looking at the marquee, which is one of the most iconic in all of the world, and really a special moment for me. So you ask the question, and I'm sitting here and can absolutely visualize what it looked like and looking at the audience. All of this is very recent in my mind's eye, and [I was] very fortunate to get this opportunity."

When the press conference was over, Maddon offered to buy a round of shots for the media. Some took him up on the offer.

Tampa Bay was not Chicago. Almost no city is in offering such a variety of things to do, places to see, and great dining experiences. And Maddon ate it up.

"The best, I really love the place. I still do. Always will. It's like a big, warm fuzzy…. I could exist there again very easily, riding my bike up and down the lake shore. But the people! Everywhere I went, I was recognized easily, a lot of kind words. There are places that are near and dear to my heart. Of course, I talk about Hazleton [Pennsylvania, where Maddon grew up], but Chicago is right up there, man!"

Maddon joined a team on the rise with such young players as Kris Bryant, Anthony Rizzo, Javier Báez, Addison Russell, and Kyle Schwarber, as well as veteran free agent pitcher Jon Lester. It was as if someone had added the ingredients for a cocktail, and all it needed was to be shaken.

"I'm so pleased with that first year. And look at the roster and all the people who came through. It's interesting how all that came together. In the beginning of the year at spring training, I was eager to get started. There were still a lot of question marks, and in spring training there was a lot going on I didn't like. I remember one day I got upset at the team about cutoff throws…I thought it was too cavalier. I think it was that point for me, the group was kind of content being the Cubs playing at Wrigley Field. It's going to get sold out no matter how we do or not do."

The Cubs were 10 games over .500 in early August 2015 when they completed a four-game sweep of the San Francisco Giants at Wrigley Field. From there, the Cubs went 35-17, yet still finished third in the very competitive National League Central. One of the big reasons for the Cubs' success was Jake Arrieta, a pitcher they acquired from the Baltimore Orioles in 2013. He went 10-5 in 2014, but no one could have foreseen what came next. He went 22-6 and won the Cy Young Award. After the All-Star break, he gave up just nine earned runs in 15 starts for a 0.75 ERA, the lowest ever for a second half of a season. Arrieta shut out the 98-win Pittsburgh Pirates in the wild-card game, then the Cubs beat the 100-win Cardinals three games to one to advance to the NLCS, where they were swept by the New York Mets.

Then came the magic year of 2016. Maddon described what it was like after they had won it all.

"It was exhausting. And, you know, you're flying back, and of course there's all kinds of stuff going on. There was an option we had, a lot of guys wanted to stay out all night and get some breakfast and continue the celebration, which I passed on, since I had nothing left in the tank. But it's really a great sense of satisfaction, like nothing you ever experienced before. From a personal standpoint, you think about those things, including your parents and everybody else—your aunts, uncles, your family, wife, and kids. And you lie down on the pillow and wake up and say, we did this."

Maddon and the Cubs did it. And many Cubs fans rejoiced in a similar fashion.

"I knew we were going to have a parade, but I had no idea it would be that kind of magnitude. I got a phone call from President Obama, because his wife Michelle was such a big Cubs fan growing up. And I had a T-shirt made: 'All Your Surrealisms Come True.' That's the only way I can describe it, because it's beyond dreams. It's indescribable. You live it, and then you reflect on it, but I don't know when it really sinks in."

The Cubs made the playoffs a franchise-record four consecutive seasons under Maddon, but missed the postseason in 2019, after which his contract wasn't extended. But during his time here, Maddon helped change a culture while managing to do what no other manager had done on the North Side of Chicago in 108 years. After he departed, the Cubs would begin another rebuild, trading Bryant, Rizzo, and Báez, while allowing Schwarber to leave.

Maddon will forever be remembered as the manager who ended the longest World Series drought in major league history.

# Ozzie Guillen

HE IS candid, controversial, and foul-mouthed; he's a champion, devoted family man, popular TV host, and critic of his home country... and much more. Meet Ozzie Guillen, if you don't already know who he is. The former manager of the Chicago White Sox, who guided them to their first World Series title in 88 years, remains a lightning rod for devoted fans and even ones who don't care for the Sox. As an analyst on NBC Sports Chicago's coverage of the team, Guillen pulls no punches, and never has. This is who he's always been, a mouth attached to a brain that's built like a high-speed train.

Oswaldo José Guillén Barrios grew up in Caracas, Venezuela, and came to the United States in 1980 as a 16-year-old on a quest to become a big-league shortstop. He was traded to the Sox by the San Diego Padres in 1984. In his first season on the South Side of Chicago, he was named American League Rookie of the Year. He would go on to play 13 of his 16 seasons with the Sox. Guillen then became a coach for the Montreal Expos and, in 2002, the Florida Marlins, who went on to win the World Series the next year (going through the Cubs to do it). One year later, he became the manager of the Sox, which included a career full of excitement, controversy, and plenty of tasty if not outrageous quotes and sound bites. He led the Sox to a championship in 2005, but they made the playoffs only once more during his rather storied eight-year run with the team. The Marlins hired him as manager in 2012, but they went 69–93, and his praise of Cuban dictator Fidel Castro got him fired despite having three years left on his contract. Guillen has been an analyst for NBC Sports Chicago since 2019.

I first met Ozzie the day he debuted as the Sox shortstop. He was this rail-thin, 21-year-old with a mustache who spoke broken English but loved to talk. He was tough to understand at times, but the more I heard him talk, the more I got used to it. Thankfully, nothing has changed, although his English has gotten a bit better. He was a dynamic player—an excellent fielder and a good contact hitter. The fans loved him, and the media glommed onto him often. But it's when he became manager that Ozzie really let loose, and I'm talking some very salty language. (Salty was his third language after Spanish and English.) I also remember a time when I had been away from the park for a year. When I returned, I decided not to be part of the media pregame scrum. I was standing about 50 feet away, and Ozzie caught me out of the corner of the eye. He gave me the middle finger, and I felt relieved. It was actually his sign of endearment! I have to say I've met a whole lot of people during the course of my half-century in this industry, and Ozzie is right up there as one of the most fascinating and enjoyable characters I've ever dealt with.

*Ozzie Guillen with the author*

Nothing changed during our interview. He was open to all subjects and not afraid to offer his thoughts, some in his third language. But Ozzie recalled just how he became manager of the Sox when they had already chosen one.

"To be honest, I know for a fact," he claimed. "During my first organization meeting with them, I knew Cito Gaston *was* the manager! Before that night, I had dinner with Jerry Reinsdorf when the Cubs were playing the Marlins [Guillen was their third-base coach in 2003]. It was, how you doing, great, boom boom, how you look at the team? Just a regular dinner. We had another dinner, nothing about baseball. All of a sudden, Jeff Torborg [who managed the White Sox for three years when Guillen was a player] called Jerry and said, 'You should listen to Ozzie, because Ozzie's running this ballclub.'"

The Marlins, who had fired Torborg as manager 38 games into the season, then called on the retired and 72-year-old Jack McKeon to manage. Guillen thought Torborg might have called Reinsdorf because he was angry he was fired and wanted to relate to the Sox chairman that Guillen was the de facto manager of the Marlins.

"Then Jerry wanted [GM] Kenny Williams to interview me. Back then, you had to wait until the World Series was over to interview managerial candidates. Williams said, 'Can we talk?' and I said, 'No problem.' I no say anything to anybody, I don't get excited—'Oh, my God, they're going to talk to me about managing the team!' I played with Kenny for a little while."

Then Guillen spread his feathers.

"I put it this way, no, no, no. Kenny played with me—that's the way to put it. I no play with Kenny—Kenny played with me."

I laughed, which happened often during our 90-minute session.

Guillen left the next day for Chicago and his meeting with Williams. "Then the interview is over. Then we celebrated winning the World Series, and I had never been in a parade in my life. I went to the parade, and I was shitfaced, oh, my God! I went to Pudge Rodríguez's house and party and party, and he said, 'Remember, you got to go to talk to the White Sox.' I said, 'Ah, I don't know.' I woke up the next day, and Pudge said, 'You have to go to the White Sox.' I went there, and I don't know how we land. I went to the hotel, and I don't remember how I checked in. I don't remember anything."

Clearly, Guillen was a tad hungover.

"I sit with Kenny and Jerry, and the first thing come out of my mouth—I don't know if it was stupid or not—I said, 'Is this meeting for real? I'm not wasting my time. I'm having a great time coaching in Miami.' And Kenny said, 'Oh, is that the way we're going to start?' I said, 'No, I'm just being honest with you. Don't do this because of a check mark—I talk to a Latino.' And then we talk. Do I tell you what we say? No! He talked to me about baseball, baseball, baseball. I leave back to Miami, and Pudge asked how it went, and I said, 'Honestly, I don't remember.' He said, 'Why you don't remember?' And I said, 'I was hungover!'"

There was a reason Guillen didn't tell Rodríguez what really happened. He recalled how the end of the meeting went. "Kenny had to go to Atlanta for a wedding, but Jerry said, 'You're going to be the manager of the White Sox.'"

"Wow!" exclaimed Guillen. "I don't know if I was shocked or anything, but I just got quiet. And Jerry says, 'You're not excited?' I said, 'Well, I don't know, not really. You just gave me a job with a lot of responsibilities, and I know how Chicago people are. I know the fans, I know the media. It's not going to be easy. That's why I'm not going to get excited. Why should I be excited?'"

But Guillen was excited to manage the team he loved. Then he discussed his contract with Williams. He was then told by Reinsdorf not to say anything to anyone. So Guillen headed back to Miami.

"I went home, and I didn't tell my wife!"

Rodríguez kept asking him what had happened. Guillen knew he was going to be the manager but wanted to honor Reinsdorf's request. Then came the press conference introducing Guillen, and eventually Rodríguez knew why Guillen couldn't say anything. But his lifestyle was about to change.

"I'm going to miss being in Miami. I was living in my house right on the beach about 10 minutes from the ballpark."

That said, Guillen was thrilled to be named the new manager of the White Sox.

"I was numb during the press conference. It was a great moment for me and my wife. From the first day to the last day, managing was outstanding. A lot of ups and downs, but I remember the ups. My family enjoyed it. The reason we still live in Chicago was because of that. My grandkids are going to grow up here. I can never degrade wearing that uniform."

As I mentioned earlier, Guillen is one of the great characters I've dealt with. I remember covering another iconic player's press conference when he was named to run a team. I was there when George Halas turned to Mike Ditka to run his Chicago Bears. And like Guillen, he won a championship, Super Bowl XX. And like Guillen, he was also bold and never afraid to speak his mind.

# *Dave Wills*

IT WAS the morning of March 5, 2023. I was in Tucson, Arizona, when I received a phone call telling me Dave Wills had died. My reaction was like many others.

*"What?"*

I was stunned. I had just texted Dave a week earlier to help promote my podcast with Joe Maddon. He gladly did, which was his nature. I was heartbroken to hear the news. What happened and why? Wills had a heart condition, which kept him from doing the play-by-play for the Tampa Bay Rays during the final two weeks of the 2022 regular season. He had just done a spring training game the day before this tragic event, went home, wasn't feeling well, and died in his sleep.

It didn't feel real.

It still doesn't.

The reaction was swift on social media, and it was nationwide, but much of it was from his hometown of Chicago. "Shocking" was what many said at first and then praise for him as a professional and person. Wills was admired, respected, and liked by everyone. He grew up here in the south suburb of Oak Lawn. Sports and broadcasting ran through his veins. He pitched for Elmhurst College. He began his Chicago career where I did, SportsPhone. He did play-by-play for UIC (University of Illinois-Chicago) basketball. He was the voice of the Kane County Cougars, a minor league baseball team. But Wills was a diehard White Sox fan and fulfilled his lifelong dream of being part of the team's broadcast crew, doing the pre- and postgame shows for 11 years. He also filled in doing some play-by-play. At age 40, he became one of the radio voices of the Rays, along with Andy Freed, and the two worked together until his untimely death 18 years later.

I aired Dave's podcast in June 2022. I knew him from his early days, and he was this ebullient fellow, always positive and seemingly always happy. How could you not like him? He never felt better than working with the White Sox. It brought such joy to his life.

What I loved the most is that he grew up with Lou Canellis, also a guest on my podcast and a longtime TV sports reporter and anchor in Chicago. The two met in kindergarten, became fast friends, and lived together as they began their careers here. And it was Canellis who helped Dave get the White Sox gig.

But Dave wanted more. He wanted to be the lead voice of a major league team, so he set out to meet that goal. First, he attempted to get the Kansas City Royals job.

"The Royals job was at the end of the 1997 season," he said. "Applied for it, got a call, went out to Kansas City, and met with the broadcast coordinator, the sports director, the program director, the radio station, had lunch at Royals Stadium. As we were driving back from the ballpark, the program director told me, 'You have a one-year-old daughter, so you're probably going to want to live in this area, it's close to the airport and close to the ballpark.'"

So, of course, Wills was thinking he'd gotten the job.

"I get back home, and about a week later, get the phone call, and the guy says, 'Well, you got the silver medal.'"

This was another way of saying he finished second, which was no different from finishing last. So Wills stayed with the White Sox for a few more years, and then came the next opportunity.

"In December of 2004, I got a phone call from Mitch Rosen, now program director for WSCR [670] The Score, who was doing some agent work at the time. He got in touch with John Brown, who had been with the White Sox but was now with the Devil Rays [who by 2008 were called simply the Rays], and John was inquiring about some guys who wanted to apply for the Devil Rays job."

So Wills' name came up as he was in Wilmington, North Carolina, doing UIC basketball, and that's where the Devil Rays official said they wanted him to apply for the job. Wills replied, "Okay, let me think about it." Dave did two games and came back to Chicago.

"And I thought to myself, *There are only 30 of these gigs in the world!* I know the Devil Rays aren't a great team right now, and the other thing that was leaning on me, though, was my wife and I had just purchased a house in Orland Park, three blocks from her older sister, three blocks from her younger sister, and a mile from her mom. And before anyone starts joking, 'Aren't you dying to get out of that area?' I loved that her mom was—if every mother-in-law was like her mom, there wouldn't be mother-in-law jokes. And her sisters are tremendous."

Now Wills is facing quite a decision. What if the Rays offer him the job, then what?

"We took this house, knocked it down to the studs, and we built it back up to all of our specifications. And I remember her brother in-law, who built the house, saying, 'Are you going to be here for two years or 30 years?' I said, 'Tom, we're not moving! This is our dream house.' We finally move into it in October, and this is December, and I'm hearing about the Devil Rays job."

Now you're getting a better idea of the predicament Wills found himself in.

"I sat on it for a week, finally sent [an audition tape] in, and it turned out I was late. And I heard the story later on they had just convened their group and lowered the number of tapes down from 300 to the final 10. About five minutes later, the mail guy comes by and said, 'Hey ah, I think this is for you, it might be another CD.'"

It so happened the guy was a member of the group who had picked the final 10. He popped the CD into the machine, listened, and called the group back together again.

"He said, 'I think you guys might want to listen to this, because I think he's as good as the final 10 that we have here.' And sure enough, I became the 11th of the final 10 and then went in for the interview.... I had left Chicago on a Thursday night after doing a UIC game and—there were two inches of snow coming down on a Friday—land in Tampa. It's 75 degrees and sunny. It's mid-January, and I'm thinking to myself, *Wow, this is nice.*"

Wills came back that evening and then had to drive up to Green Bay. "There's a white-out the next morning, and I'm thinking to myself, *I don't think they have to worry about this in Florida.*"

It took about a week to 10 days for Wills to get the call back from the Devil Rays.

"I remember getting the call on February 1. It was 10:00 o'clock in the morning. I was vacuuming my family room, answered the call, they offer me the gig."

Wills drove out to Grandstand, a sporting goods store, which was near Guaranteed Rate Field (then named U.S. Cellular Field) and was a big sponsor of Wills', and wondered if they had a Devil Rays jacket and hat?

"They did. Grabbed it, told 'em what happened, drove to my wife's office, and walked into her office with a Devils Ray hat and jacket, and she said, 'You're being a bit presumptuous, aren't you?' I said, 'Nope. I got the job.' And she started crying, and I think for most of the rest of the day, because she wasn't ready to move. But after everything had kind of worked out, and coming down here and looking for housing, I remember one time pulling into our garage, and she looked at the snow blower and the shovels, and she said, 'I guess we're not going to need those again.' And that's when I knew, no pun intended, she was warming up to the idea."

I asked Dave if he'd ever consider returning to the White Sox, and his answer was reinforced by how much his wife really had warmed to sunny Tampa Bay.

"She kind of jokingly once said, 'If that did happen, you would be going without me.'"

Now his wife and two kids are without Dave, as are all of us.

# Pat Hughes

HE'S IN the Hall of Fame. In July 2023, longtime Cubs play-by-play announcer Pat Hughes was named the recipient of the Ford C. Frick Award, the highest honor awarded to broadcasters by the National Baseball Hall of Fame. Gifted with an excellent and melodic voice, Hughes has been calling major league baseball since 1983. He spent the first year of his career with the Minnesota Twins and the next 12 years calling Milwaukee Brewers games. He's been with the Cubs since 1996, and for many of those years with the immensely popular Hall of Famer Ron Santo. Since Santo's death in 2010, Hughes worked with Keith Moreland and for the last 10 years, Ron Coomer. Hughes is like your favorite easy-chair, comfortable and inviting. But when the situation warrants, he can shift into high gear, demonstrating an almost innate ability to carry the moment. Hughes has been behind the mic for some historic moments, including the Cubs' first World Series title in 108 years, two no-hitters by Jake Arrieta, groundbreaking home runs by Sammy Sosa, and many more.

Hughes is the epitome of professionalism in his handling of a broadcast. He always opens it with, "This is Pat Hughes reporting," and does that as well as anyone in the business. He also blends in a quick wit that brings laughter to the booth. He also brought out the best in Santo, who himself could make an audience laugh with some of his comments and stories. Hughes' years with Santo are some of the most memorable in Chicago broadcast history.

Every major league announcer has his own home run call, and Hughes has delivered a measured and exciting one for many years: "It's got a chaaaance...gone!" Or, for the no-doubters: "Take out the tape measure...long gone!"

Hughes has been named Illinois Sportscaster of the Year nine times and was honored with the Ring Lardner Award for excellence in sports journalism. He's also produced *Baseball Voices,* audio tributes to some of the game's finest baseball announcers.

Hughes has also dealt with throat issues. He's undergone three surgeries in a span of three years for dysplasia, a rare precancerous growth on his vocal cords that affects only some 10,000 people worldwide. So far, the voice has held up, but Hughes says there's a likelihood he'll need more surgery down the road.

Pat is a great storyteller and he's told plenty about Santo. I would pay him a visit in the Wrigley Field booth from time to time and not only enjoy his company but that of Santo's and Coomer's. He's outgoing, friendly, and a joy to spend time with, especially in the Cubs cafeteria, where the stories can flow.

If you think Pat's greatest moment in the booth was calling the final out of the World Series, think again.

"It was Game 6 of the National League Championship Series of 2016," he said, "the Kyle Hendricks masterpiece against the Dodgers. The win that put the Cubs into the World Series. Cubs fans certainly, instantly recall that game, but it was dwarfed by the enormity of the World Series championship 10 days later. You have to backpedal and realize the Cubs had not won a National League pennant in 71 years! So that was a gigantic win."

What I remember most about that game, as a reporter, was being allowed on the field about 15 minutes after the Cubs won. The crowd was deafening. I had never been on the field when a full house of fans was screaming at the top of its lungs, and it was a glorious, ear-piercing sound I will never forget.

"Hendricks was at the top of his game," as Hughes recalled that Game 6. "I think he gave up one or two hits in 7⅔ innings [it was two]. The Cubs roughed up Clayton Kershaw with some great offensive work early in the game.... Anthony Rizzo homered. So did Willson Contreras. The Cubs won the game 5–0, but it didn't even seem that close. It seemed like it was 25–0."

After the final out, Hughes remained quiet for about 25 seconds. He let the crowd roar, and, as I mentioned about my experience on the field, boy, did they roar! Even Hughes admitted it was the loudest he's ever heard Wrigley Field in the time he has been with the Cubs.

"I was so emotional at that moment to say 'the National League–champion Chicago Cubs.' I really had to concentrate on not breaking up and really losing it emotionally. And I tell people, if there's ever going to be a greater moment than Game 7 of the World Series, it will be that day when the Cubs win the World Series at Wrigley Field in front of the best fans in the universe."

Of course, this Game 7 was played in Cleveland, a nerve-wracking contest after the Cubs had battled back from a three-games-to-one Series deficit.

"In the back of my mind, I wanted to say, 'The Chicago Cubs win the World Series,' which is exactly what I did say. But you have to backpedal because you don't want to get too far ahead of yourself. As a radio man, it's different than a guy on television. A baseball game can end in any number of ways. Let's take two scenarios: In Game 7 the Cubs beat the Indians 11–0. Or the other scenario, which is exactly what happened. It was cliffhanger, back and forth, nerve-wracking, 10 innings of drama, wall to wall. So, if you tried to be real fancy and creative and thought of something real clever to say, it may be very appropriate for the cliffhanger but not appropriate at all for the blowout game."

Fortunately for Hughes, but perhaps not as fortunate for Cubs fans, who were on pins and needles for hours, the game was nerve-wracking.

"I decided I didn't want to be the story. The story was the Chicago Cubs finally, after 108 seasons, winning the World Series. That was the story, and I wanted to be true to my audience on the final play, which I think I did. I was very proud to have said, 'A little bouncer slowly toward Bryant...' so I got the slow bouncer in there. And then I said, 'he will glove it and throw to Rizzo...' which was an unusual way to call it."

Usually, Hughes will say something like, "There's a ground ball to third, Bryant up with it, the toss across in time for out number two."

"But I waited until I saw the signal from umpire Joe West. I saw Bryant slip as he made the throw and Rizzo reach up for the throw, and I knew if he caught it we would be in business."

Hughes then got a glimpse of Ben Zobrist running in from left field and, as he saw the final play, jump up and down. Cubs fans everywhere around the world were jumping up and down. Their team finally ended the longest championship drought in American sports history. And Pat Hughes was there to call it.

As nerve-wracking as that game was, there was another nerve-wracking event that took place after Hughes did a road broadcast of a Northwestern basketball game. It was a not-so-happy landing in Happy Valley.

"It was going to be Northwestern against Penn State. We were going to play on a Saturday, so Friday night, we fly in and it's the winter. It was blowing snow and windy like you couldn't believe. Horrendous conditions. It was a charter plane, not one of the big airliners that have multiple stewardesses and co-pilots. We had a pilot and a co-pilot and maybe one stewardess, and it was one of those planes that seated about 30 people. I remember we tried to land in Happy Valley, Pennsylvania, and it was too windy, and you could feel the plane shaking and swaying back and forth, which is not a good feeling when you're going to fly and land in a snowstorm."

The way Hughes was describing this, I started picturing an Alfred Hitchcock movie. The pilot couldn't land.

"So the pilot tried again, and the same thing happened. He had to abort and go back up in the air and try it again. This cycle repeated itself five or six times, and each one that is unsuccessful you become increasingly uncomfortable. And finally, on the sixth or seventh try, the wind had calmed down enough and the pilot understood the conditions well enough to try and make a landing, and he did. He did a very nice job, and it was smooth and there were no issues. But I remember the players, these young athletes spontaneously erupted in a cheer! They were giving the pilot a standing ovation. They were laughing and high-fiving. It was one of the worst flights I'd ever been on."

I think we can commiserate with Hughes.

One thing's for certain: Hughes has taken us on some mighty exciting rides during his times with the Cubs, and for now this Ford C. Frick Award-winning broadcaster has no plans of permanently landing his career.

# *Paul Sullivan*

IF I'M writing a chapter about someone I interviewed for the podcast, why not write about someone who writes for a living? Paul Sullivan does that, and better than just about anyone else. Since he walked in the door at the *Chicago Tribune* more than 40 years ago, Sullivan has spent most of his time writing sports and, in particular, baseball. Whether it was the Cubs or Sox, "Sully," as he's affectionately known, has chronicled thousands of games as a beat writer, many more that wound up in the loss column. He's done so in a professional if not biting manner. He was tossing opinions into his stories long before it became the vogue for beat writers to do so. Now he has free rein as the proprietor of the newspaper's historic sports column, "In the Wake of the News."

But for those many years reporting from the North and South Sides of town and when he was traveling on the road, Sullivan spent endless hours making sure he got the story right. And his stories were always must-reads because of the facts he delivered and the confrontations he had with certain players and management. Sullivan admitted he could piss off people with what he wrote, but seldom would any reader argue it wasn't true.

Perhaps what's most interesting about Sullivan's award-winning career—he's been named Illinois Sportswriter of the Year three times and received the prestigious Ring Lardner Award for excellence in sports journalism—is the fact he wasn't allowed into the University of Missouri's highly rated journalism school. He claimed to have fooled around too much in his early days in college and didn't meet the requirements. But before he managed to find his way to the *Tribune*, the diminutive Sullivan (he stands 5′5″) worked as a bell boy at the famous Drake Hotel in downtown Chicago. He carried Bill Cosby's bags, got some Q-tips for Sophia Loren, and actually made the cut in the movie *Continental Divide*, starring the late John Belushi. It was a short scene but memorable enough that the Glenwood Theater, where Sullivan had ushered, put on its marquee "Belushi and Sullivan."

*Paul Sullivan and John Belushi* (Photograph courtesy of Paul Sullivan)

When Sullivan did manage to get a job at the *Tribune*, he eventually became a leg man for the legendary news columnist Mike Royko. From there, it was on to sports and the baseball beat.

I first met Sully in one of the ballpark press conferences, and right away I knew he was different from a cluster of the other writers, many of whom either loathed, scolded, or ignored the electronic media, which had grown exponentially in the 1980s. Sully welcomed us, treated us with dignity, and even wrote about us. Yes, he wrote about me when I lost my job at WBBM in July 2020. It almost read as a professional obituary, but it was also an incredibly kind gesture by Sully, who may be small in build but has a heart bigger than you might imagine. He has a self-deprecating sense of humor but his feistiness is both endearing and respected among the members of the media. Sully is a favorite in bars (he's attended his share) and can share stories with the best of them. He may not be a favorite of some of the people he writes about, but he's definitely a favorite among the legion of readers he has.

I've watched Sully ply his trade. He doesn't try to be controversial during interviews, but some of his stories and columns have resulted in bad blood between him and those he wrote about. Reading him skewering former Cubs general manager Ed Lynch, whom he wrote should be fired, or White Sox Hall of Fame slugger Frank Thomas (both men were well over 6' tall and towered over Sully) was admirable and thoroughly enjoyable. Since Sully mainly covered the Cubs, I'm going to focus on two particular players—two very talented, temperamental and controversial players—Carlos Zambrano and Sammy Sosa. First, Zambrano, whom Sully dubbed "Big Z," and with whom he had a rather fractured and celebrated relationship.

"Oh my Gosh," an exasperated Sullivan said. "Big Z had quite a few incidents that were beyond the pale. There was shouting, screaming, throwing things, smashing things with a bat! So it was my job to chronicle this. I said, hey, this guy acts like an idiot. He's a good pitcher, but he acts like a fool, and it's a bad example for kids."

Sully's run-ins with Zambrano became legendary and, at times, comical. You have to picture this—Zambrano stood 6'4" and weighed 275 pounds. He was not only an intimidating pitcher but an intimidating person, as well. I know because I had a run-in with him, too, and I stand 5′7″!

"So one day we were in Milwaukee soon after they opened the new ballpark [April 6, 2001]. We're near the batting cage, and he picked me up like a sack of potatoes and held me over his head!"

Oh, if only we had a picture of this. Sully agreed and wished he had one, too.

"Z, put me down, you're going to injure yourself. I'm going to get blamed."

This is when the Cubs were still in the division race and had a good team.

"He did put me down and we had a good laugh about it."

If you think this is the end of the story, think again.

"He also, once up in Milwaukee, [offered] one of the security guards...$100,000 to kill me!"

At this point I was beyond incredulous.

"He didn't know what to say and [said], 'I can't do that.' I was standing right there and said, 'Thanks, man.' That's the kind of relationship we had. We had some fun with one another. Everyone thought we hated each other because we did yell at each other a lot of times because he would be mad at me for something I wrote. I actually liked him as a person. I thought he was funny, but he was a bad example for kids."

During the 2007 season, the temperamental Zambrano punched teammate Michael Barrett in the face in the dugout, sending the catcher to the hospital. It's there for anyone to see on YouTube. But Zambrano, once out of baseball, changed his ways.

"I saw him at the Cubs Convention right before the pandemic. We looked at each other like, 'Whoa, are we going to talk to each other?'"

They did.

"I interviewed him, and he was a minister now and he totally changed. He sent me a message thanking me. I think we're okay now after all these years."

The same might not be said of another Cubs star, Sammy Sosa, even though Sully has an open mind.

"That's very complicated," explained Sully about his relationship with Sosa. "There was a time where Sammy looked at me as his biographer. During the home run race [between Sosa and Mark McGwire in 1998], I was writing so much good stuff about him. Then came the steroid issue, the corked bat, and walking out on the team. It really had a bad ending with the Cubs."

Sosa was suspended eight games for using a corked bat in 2003, and on the final day of the 2004 season, he left the game early and was fined $87,400. Later, Mark McGwire and other players admitted to taking steroids. Sosa and others were accused of taking them, too, though Sosa has always denied it.

"And we had a bad ending, too. I remember he once came up to me and said, 'You don't like me, I don't like you, so I'll just say, *bleep* you...you just say *bleep* me, and let's move on.' So I said, 'Cool!' That lasted for two weeks. He loafed on some play, and I had to write about it, and then he was back to hating me again."

Not exactly what you would call a cordial relationship, but Sosa had an ego bigger than his head, which had doubled in size between the end of the 1997 season and spring training in 1998. The assumption started to build that Sosa was on some kind of performance-enhancing drugs. Sully has never voted for Sosa for the Hall of Fame but believes he should be honored by the Cubs organization.

"I do think he should be in the Cubs Hall of Fame. I advocate that and I think he should return to Wrigley Field, even though there are a lot of people who don't like him. But there's still a lot of people who do. Barry Bonds is welcomed in San Francisco, McGwire is welcomed in St. Louis."

Sully doesn't believe anyone totally forgives the steroid guys, but he does believe Sosa should be welcomed back to Wrigley Field. "Sosa did contribute a lot to the organization, especially financially. They made a lot of money off him."

The two years prior to the 1998 season, the Cubs averaged 2.2 million fans. During that year's home run chase, attendance increased by more than 400,000, and went up by about 200,000 more the next season and stayed around that level for the next two seasons, when Sosa averaged 59 homers.

"I think they should invite him back."

I was delighted to invite Sully to my podcast.

# Jesse Rogers

JESSE ROGERS climbed a lot of ladders to get to where he is today. For a sports-rabid kid growing up in the northern suburbs of Chicago to becoming a national baseball writer/reporter and on-air personality for ESPN, Rogers put his stamp of excellence and professionalism wherever he's worked. He was a 23-year-old when thrust into the role of producer for the *Monsters of the Midday*, the original pairing of Mike North and Dan Jiggetts at 670 The Score. Rogers parlayed that into guest hosting, to becoming the pre- and postgame host for Chicago Blackhawks broadcasts. He was also my cohost when we debuted *Hit and Run*, a weekend baseball program in 2005 that is still running today. Rogers was also program director for the ill-fated Chicago Sports Webio Internet project that not long after its debut in April 2009 came crashing down because the man funding it was doing so through a Ponzi scheme. But it didn't take Rogers long to bounce back. He was hired by ESPN to cover the surging Chicago Blackhawks and then, in 2015, was switched to the surging Cubs. During the Cubs run in the late 2010s, Rogers cowrote a book about then manager Joe Maddon called *Try Not to Suck*. Then in 2021, ESPN's lead baseball reporter, Pedro Gomez, died suddenly. It thrust Rogers into yet another position, as Gomez's replacement.

Jesse and I bonded rather quickly despite our age difference, some 14 years. Part of the reason is Jesse's down-to-earth personality. He's simply a very nice guy. We covered the 1997 NCAA men's Final Four in Indianapolis, driving back after the championship game at 2:30 in the morning. Jesse made great time driving.

Several years later, he joined our poker group and fit in like a glove. When I did a solo baseball show in 2004, I requested the program director add Jesse. It was one of the smartest moves I made.

Jesse helped make the show much more enjoyable, as we both contributed to different segments.

Jesse is a big hockey fan, but before getting the national assignment to cover the Blackhawks, he was named the pre- and postgame host for 670 The Score, which carried the radio broadcasts.

"My first day on the job was 9/11," he recalled. "It was the opening of training camp."

What's interesting to note is the Blackhawks current play-by-play voice on radio, John Wiedeman, got a similar gig with the New York Islanders in 2001, and the day he drove into the city to rent a van to move into an apartment also just happened to be 9/11.

Jesse remembers that day vividly. "I'm going to the first day of training camp at the United Center, and I'm ready to report the hell out of the Blackhawks. They had no following other than the die-hards. They were off the radar in Chicago in the 2000s. So I go to the United Center that day, and they send me home. I'm living in a high-rise in Chicago, and I'm just staring at the Sears Tower [now Willis Tower] all day praying for myself and everyone else that nothing happens in Chicago."

Luckily, nothing happened, but for those of us who remember, it was a shocking, eye-opening, and somber time in the country.

Rogers was the Hawks' pre- and postgame host for a number of years, then did some other things until the local ESPN station came calling. "When the Hawks got good, it was a decade since anyone cared, and there weren't many people in the sports media business who knew hockey. It's a very specialized game. Even some fans don't know all the rules. I knew it because I played it and did the pre- and postgame. WMVP-ESPN 1000 was looking for a reporter, and I called suggesting they hire a producer who I knew. They said, 'What are you going to do right now?' ESPN was expanding. 'So the Hawks are getting good, and we're expanding our base of reporters. We need a hockey reporter—how would you like to do it?'"

Jesse jumped at the idea, having already been the pre- and postgame host at the competing station. Jesse took the job without knowing its ramifications.

"I did not it would entail full-time, going to every road game. I did not know what they were really asking. So I became the beat reporter for ESPN Chicago. Those three to four years, and leading up to the championship and afterward, honestly, were the best times of my career because of the lifestyle—summers off, two and a half hour games, and they don't play every day."

Jesse also had three young children at the time, so the summer gave him a chance to be with them more. He also started covering for ESPN the network. "Then they win that championship, and the highlight of them all was being on the players' bus during the parade, tickertape down Michigan Avenue, and I can't believe I was there. It was an amazing run. It was a career highlight, it really was."

But Jesse had another career highlight, only this was with the Cubs and during a rather paralyzing time in the country. "I was the sideline reporter during the pandemic season of 2020, when the Cubs won the division and hosted the Miami Marlins in the postseason. Nobody was allowed in Wrigley Field. The announcers for that game, Jon "Boog" Sciambi [current TV voice of the Cubs] and Chipper Jones were in Bristol, Connecticut [where the ESPN campus is]. I was asked to be the sideline reporter—the only person in the stands. I couldn't get near the field. This game was on ABC-TV nationally."

It was truly a lucky break for Jesse. "Here I am as a Cubs fan, growing up and covering the team, and now being asked to be a sideline reporter for a playoff game. So there I am in the stands doing a report in the third inning, and I get a text on my phone."

The studio had been texting Jesse, what with reporters in different parts of the country. They had been texting one another to stay on top of the things.

"I get a text, and I think it's from one of them, but it was from my sweet, sweet 14-year-old daughter at the time, Carly. I'm reading this verbatim: 'Dad, are you busy? I just printed something in the basement. Can you go get it?' My career moment on ABC-TV, and my daughter couldn't care less!"

Funny story from a funny, loving, and caring guy I call a good friend.

# Jason Benetti

JASON BENETTI is part of the new breed of broadcasters, an august group including the likes of Adam Amin, Chris Vosters, Cassidy Hubbarth, and Joe Davis (the lead voice at Fox, who replaced the legendary Vin Scully in the L.A. Dodgers broadcast booth), to name a few. Benetti burst onto the scene as the TV voice of the Chicago White Sox, replacing the venerable Ken "Hawk" Harrelson. He had an instant impact on viewers and his partner, Steve Stone, the longtime analyst for the Chicago White Sox and, before that, the crosstown Cubs. Benetti and Stone's partnership has blossomed into one of the most enjoyable duos anywhere. They play off one another's expertise, along with, at times, a devilish sense of humor.

Benetti actually began his career at Homewood-Flossmoor High School, which boasted a robust radio department. The school has also produced a bevy of Chicago sports journalists, including the *Chicago Tribune*'s Paul Sullivan, MLB.com reporter Scott Merkin, 670 The Score host Laurence Holmes, NBC Sports Chicago's Chuck Garfien, and WGN-TV news anchor Ben Bradley. From there, Benetti became sports director at the prestigious Newhouse School of Public Communications at Syracuse University. This led him to jobs with ESPN and Fox Sports, which has resulted in a very hectic schedule for the 39-year-old Benetti.

I got to know Jason while covering the Sox. I would drop into the broadcast booth to say hello and was always greeted graciously by him and Stone, and of course, there was a comedic line or two thrown in. It was so easy to tell that Jason loves his job. There was an air of pleasure watching him work so seamlessly with Stone. But Jason also works well with so many others, including the sage and artful Bill Raftery, and the iconic, if not off-the-wall, Bill Walton.

I found Jason to be refreshingly open and sincere. It's a quality that is so endearing. During our thoroughly engrossing interview, Jason discussed cerebral palsy. He'd been born 10 weeks premature and spent three months in the hospital, where complications led to his diagnosis of the disorder, which wasn't discovered until he was a toddler. While it has created issues growing up, Jason began by focusing on his loving parents, who created a world full of possibilities for him.

"My parents went through a lot when I was sick and growing up," he told me. "And their beauty is that it wasn't the center of my universe. Whether that leads me to being naïve about it when I was young, maybe, but there was never any idea like, oh, you can't do this, but you can do this but shouldn't do that. I played basketball with my friends growing up. We played football in the backyard, and I was big wrestling fan. And my parents were terrified when I would wrestle with my cousins, things like that, because they wouldn't want me to snap in half."

Benetti joked he is about 100 pounds now and was just seven pounds then. Benetti knows how difficult it was for his parents when he was born 10 weeks prematurely.

"It was not easy for them, especially because, when you see your kid growing up in a hospital a lot, that's hard, and you kind of want to protect it. And for me, I ended up making a lot of friends very early in life with doctors and nurses. There was one doctor I had who made an amazing Donald Duck impression. The things you remember. I remember the nurses coming in with a giant basket of syringes, and it was like, 'Time to draw blood.' And every once in a while, my mom would, like, push them away because, why do we have to do that again? It was difficult, but the great thing that comes from looking different is that, at some point over the last 10 years, I gained a substantial belief in my work and the work I put into myself. And there's no way to say it without sounding egotistical, but I'll give it a run: I know I'm good at what I do because if I wasn't, no one would put me on television."

Benetti has a lazy eye and also walks with a limp. None of that now appears to hinder his meteoric rise to fame, but it did have an affect growing up. "I became a psych major in college, but I was not before that. I was naïve to it at first. I think it went in stages. I know I have to wear these braces, and I know I wear casts after surgeries. I didn't know the alternatives. There was no Internet for me to know that kids didn't spend their summers in bed rehabbing. Then in middle school and high school, people would say stuff, and I would get mad about it, but I wouldn't lash out and I kept it in."

But Benetti didn't want to be deterred from doing TV despite his disability.

"I became fearful in college and beyond, in that I could get however good as I wanted to get, and somebody might say, 'We just don't want to put you on TV.' And so I wanted to make sure that wasn't going to happen. I was angry about looking different, and I was angry about the way I was treated sometimes because it felt wrong to me."

In college, Benetti became the sports director at the college radio station, and the day he got the job, his friends were very excited. Later on in his tenure, he would give out assignments and would choose who went to and covered the Big East Tournament. But on AOL Instant Messenger at the time, one of Benetti's peers, who didn't like him because he didn't give him a certain assignment, put up as an away message, "At least he'll be a great story for somebody's magazine one day."

"It was just a shot because I walk funny? That stuff kinds of sticks with you. And I will say, I have gotten a little more graceful and giving myself license to get frustrated sometimes, because when you walk the earth looking different every day...that bubbles a little bit, and it's frustrating. But I will say I have derived a lot of joy and confidence from the idea this career has worked out despite what I look like."

I wondered whether, growing up, Benetti was teased or even bullied and would get fed up and say, enough is enough!

"Yeah, it happens a lot, and people say stuff to me in coded language, I can push you around. A decision-maker told my friend about why I wasn't getting better assignments, and hoping it wasn't about his disability, and the decision-maker said, 'Oh, no, we're very understating of Jason's situation.' What the hell does that mean? Understanding of my situation? I'm a sports announcer, I'm not some charity case. I've come to the realization, the perception I get from people in the world is, it's not going to change. I meet people over and over every day who have never met someone like me or someone with a disability. I do think there are some people, and they know who they are, who see it as some sign of weakness, and that's inexplicable to me."

Benetti admits he built a wall, but added it's an understanding, as well, and that's where Benetti's sense of humor comes in. Most people mean very well to Benetti, but that doesn't mean he doesn't get irritated. He never wanted a job because he has a disability, but he also wants it known the barriers that people create.

"The universal message I try to impart is, get really good at what you do and have them say yes!"

Some people treat Benetti with fairness and respect, while others do not.

"I thought that would end in my adulthood, but it has not. And so, I generally think people are good, and I generally want to smile throughout my day, but I also realize I have to have fang sometimes to protect myself."

Benetti has cleared paths for others with disabilities to believe they can achieve success no matter the pratfalls and potholes along the way. His life has become a determined and shining example of that.

"Sports has become such a way for me to make friends and have value in society and what it's done for my life. I will always be grateful. I love going places, I love feeling the difference where my mind goes in a certain city. Just going somewhere else is inspiration for me, and I love it dearly. I know one day it won't exist anymore, and I want to do as much of the world as possible, because when your world shrinks, I think you end up not having the most fulfilling experience you can have on this earth."

It would appear Benetti is fulfilling that experience, but he has a long way to go. There are more mountains to climb, and as we've come to learn, his disability won't hinder him from climbing further and further.

# Steve Stone

IT'S HARD to believe, but Steve Stone's ties to Chicago baseball date back to 1973, when he became a pitcher for the White Sox. A half-century later, he's still with the Sox, now as their popular TV analyst, working alongside the multitalented Jason Benetti. Stone is one of baseball's preeminent analysts, gifted with the ability to call plays before they happen. Call it clairvoyance or simply a great baseball mind, Stone's acuity, combined with a sarcastic sense of humor, has made him one of the city's most popular sports figures. He was a sidekick to the incomparable Harry Caray and then Caray's grandson Chip; worked with Ken "Hawk" Harrelson until his retirement; and more recently, with Benetti. He's the only man to play and broadcast for both Chicago baseball teams.

One year after landing with the Sox in 1973, Stone was traded to the Cubs in a deal that included the immensely popular and eventual Hall of Famer Ron Santo, who carved out a career as a rather unique analyst himself. Three years later, Stone rejoined the Sox as a free agent before bolting for the Baltimore Orioles in 1979. He was a very pedestrian 78-79 in his career until 1980, when he suddenly produced an unexpected dream season with the Orioles. He went 25-7 in 1980, earning the coveted Cy Young Award as the American League's best pitcher. He also started the All-Star Game for the American league. A year later, Stone suffered shoulder tendinitis and retired to begin what would be a second and most rewarding career in the broadcast booth.

Chicago has been blessed to have outstanding commentators in the baseball broadcast booths—from Lou Boudreau to Jimmy Piersall, Ron Coomer, Tom Paciorek, Ron Santo, and others—but Stone stands alone. His ability to dissect a game while interacting with his partners earned him a nomination for the Ford C. Frick Award, given out by the Baseball Hall of Fame.

Stone's career began a year after retiring. He joined ABC's *Monday Night Baseball*. A year later, in 1983, he began an odyssey with Harry Caray, playing a seemingly perfect second fiddle to the iconic and bigger-than-life personality. Stone admitted being somewhat dwarfed by Caray, but nonetheless the partnership lasted 15 years, until Caray's death in February 1998. Caray's replacement was his grandson Chip, who came from Fox. The two worked together seven seasons before a controversial rift with the franchise helped ease both out at the end of 2004. Over the next four years, Stone worked as an analyst for sports station 670 The Score (WSCR-AM) before returning to the South Side, where he's been ever since.

Stone is an avid reader and early investor in Lettuce Entertain You, a family-owned restaurant group that debuted in 1971 and has since opened 130 restaurants. It's flagship, R.J. Grunts, remains a thriving business in Chicago's Lincoln Park neighborhood.

I first came in contact with "Stony" as a young reporter back in 1978. It was his last season with the Sox. Our relationship continued when Stony joined the Cubs broadcast booth. But when I joined WSCR in 1992, I also began covering spring training, and it was during one particular game that I had a chance to understand Stony's innate ability to be a step ahead. We were in a press box booth and chatting during a game that was not being broadcast, when suddenly he turned to me and said of the batter, "Watch him go the opposite way for a double." So, on the next pitch, the batter stroked an opposite-field double. My jaw dropped as I looked at Stony, who flashed one of those I-told-you-so smiles.

When Stony left the Cubs, I got to know him even better. He would treat me to breakfast at Nookies on Wells Street and sometimes dinner at various places, regaling me with all sorts of baseball stories while mixing in current events. He did most of the talking, as is his wont, but I didn't mind listening at all. Stony can command a conversation and never be boring.

During our entertaining interview, Stony recalled a time in 1978 when he was a member of the White Sox and had a rather interesting conversation with teammate Don Kessinger: "I'm on the back of the bus with Kessinger, and we're in Baltimore to play the Orioles. It's September, and I just sat there and looked at him and said, 'Guess who's going to manage the White Sox next year?' And he said, 'Who?' And I said, 'Guess.' So he mentioned a few names, and I said, 'Nope...nope...nope...nope.' And he said, 'Well, who?' I said, 'You!'"

Kessinger, who spent 12 of his 16 years in the majors with the Cubs but now was at the tail end of his career with the Sox, stared incredulously at Stone.

"He said, 'Me? I got one year left on my contract, then I'm going home to raise my boys. I don't want to manage.'"

As I had mentioned earlier, Stone has a reputation for being clairvoyant, but this time he might have had some inside information.

"So he said, 'What are you talking about?' And I said, 'Because you're going to manage this team next year.' He said, 'No, that's wrong. How many people know this or think this?' 'Right now, there's just two—you and me. But soon, Bill Veeck [the team owner then] is going to come to the realization you're the next guy.' So anyway, he just poo-pooed it, and that was that. So [then] we get off the road, and I got to Bill Veeck and said, 'I want you to do me a favor.' And he said, 'What's that?' I said, 'When you name Don Kessinger the manager next year, I want you to name me as the pitching coach'!"

Stone was cagey if nothing else, but didn't realize what was in store for himself.

"He said, 'You're a pitcher!' And I said, 'Yes, but he's a player, and he has one more year left on his contract.' He said, 'That's not going to happen. I'm talking to (this guy and that guy).' and I said, 'I know. And, eventually, when you talk to all of them and you name Kessinger, name me your pitching coach, because young pitchers aren't ready yet.'"

Veeck was one of baseball's most inventive souls. He was credited with planting the vines on Wrigley Field's outfield wall. He once sent Eddie Gaedel to pinch hit in a game when he was owner of the St. Louis Browns. Gaedel stood all of 3'7" tall and became the shortest player in the history of major league baseball. He drew a walk on four pitches and never played again. Veeck signed Larry Doby while owner of the Cleveland Indians in 1947, making him the second Black player in the game, following Jackie Robinson. Veeck also introduced the exploding scoreboard at old Comiskey Park in Chicago. The team still has one to this day.

Since Kessinger had one year left on his contract, Stone reminded Veeck that he once had had a player/manager in Cleveland. "'Lou Boudreau won the World Series in 1948, and he was 24 years old,'" he told him. (Boudreau was actually 31.) "'Kessinger is more mature than that. He's had a lot of experience, and he's gonna be your guy.' He says, 'He's not gonna be my guy!' I said, 'Just remember what I told you.' So anyway, time clicked along, and now we have 10 days left in the season, and Kessinger comes up to me and says, 'Hypothetically, who would you pick as a pitching coach?' And I said, 'I told you at the back of the bus as we were heading to Memorial Stadium in Baltimore, I would pick me. I'm the best guy to do that job.' He said, 'You're still pitching. You can't pick you. If you had any choice of everybody else, who are you going to pick?' I said, 'If you couldn't pick me, the guy's Fred Martin.'"

Martin is credited with teaching the split-fingered fastball to Bruce Sutter in the minor leagues. The difficult pitch to hit turned Sutter into one of the most dominant closers in the game and, eventually, a Hall of Famer.

"'He's sitting in Arizona not doing anything, and you remember him with your time with the Cubs when he was there?'" Stone continued. "I said, 'He would be the guy, but I think you're ignoring the fact that I'm better!' So he just laughed, and that was that. Two weeks after the season ended, Don Kessinger was named player/manager of the White Sox, and a couple of weeks after that, Martin was named pitching coach."

There are several postscripts to this story. Kessinger had been preceded as manager by Larry Doby, who became only the second

Black manager in major league history, following Frank Robinson. Fred Martin developed cancer and lasted just a few weeks as White Sox pitching coach, then died. Kessinger lasted just 106 games, as the Sox went 46-60. During that time, he batted .200. He was replaced by Tony La Russa, who hired Ron Schueler to replace Martin. Schueler would eventually become the team's general manager. La Russa managed the Sox until 1986, then went on to win World Series titles with the Oakland A's and St. Louis Cardinals before retiring in 2011. Then he was rehired by the Sox ahead of the 2021 season at age 76. He retired for good after the 2022 season.

As for Stone, he signed a four-year deal with the Baltimore Orioles after the 1978 season, had that incredible year to remember in 1980, retired in 1981, and soon after began a broadcast career that continues to this day with the White Sox.

# FOOTBALL

# Gary Fencik

THE MYSTIQUE surrounding the Chicago Bears' only Super Bowl championship has been fading for a number of years now. It was January 20, 1986, when the Bears pulverized the New England Patriots in New Orleans and came home to a heroes' welcome, albeit on a day in which the celebratory and frozen fans in downtown actually prevented the championship buses from actually moving through the crowd. Yet some of the members of that team remain prominent for several reasons. Tom Thayer continues to be Jeff Joniak's sidekick on Bears radio broadcasts. Dan Hampton still does a radio and TV show, while Steve McMichael's battle with ALS remains an ongoing yet sorrowful story. Jay Hilgenberg was doing Bears radio until it moved stations. Ron Rivera is head coach of the Washington Commanders.

Gary Fencik makes occasional appearances on radio but otherwise continues his role as a senior partner in an investment company. Fencik was part of a ferocious defense, arguably the best in history for a Super Bowl season that featured Hall of Famers Hampton, Richard Dent, and Mike Singletary. Fencik was a defensive back who teamed up with Doug Plank to be called "the Hit Men" because of their aggressive, hard-hitting tackles. Fencik, a Yale grad and a 10th-round pick of the Miami Dolphins in 1976, eventually became part of the early groundwork that formed this incredibly talented and entertaining team in the 1980s. And Fencik was very much part of the entertainment factor. He did several whimsical beer commercials and played a role in the famous "Super Bowl Shuffle," though his dancing left plenty to be desired. Fencik's post-playing career also included being a radio and TV analyst.

As a reporter during those wild years with the Bears, Gary was many of those go-to guys you wanted to interview. He was refreshing, honest, articulate, and embraced our roles. I would see him from time to time after his playing career, but it was at a chance meeting in a market that we decided to do this interview. It was during the COVID period when masks were required. Funny thing is, Gary recognized me with my mask on, but I wasn't sure who he was until he said hello. We had a wonderful chat, which resulted in a wonderful interview that included those 1985 Bears, why they were so dominating, and why they never won again.

"The defense certainly got a lot more credit than the offense," Fencik remembered. "I've talked to Matt Suhey [a fullback] many times. He felt if we could get up 10 points, nobody was going to catch up with us. That was a defense that was really, really consistent. We got a lot of sacks that made it easy to get turnovers, because that quarterback is probably throwing earlier than he would like."

The Bears finished 18-1 overall and only gave up more than 10 points in a game five times, yet their offense scored a franchise record 456 points!

"It was all part of a process. It just didn't happen overnight. We had kind of an awakening on the '84 team, beating Washington in Washington in the first round of the playoffs. And Todd Bell kind of changed the whole game by hitting the running back on a third-down play. I mean he crushed him, and that was kind of a wake-up bell for us. Winning that game was huge, but losing in San Francisco [quarterback Jim McMahon didn't play in either game]—we lost and didn't score a point, and we were all crying in the locker room. You know, you got that far and then [head coach Mike] Ditka had us again next year. The first time we met, he basically said, we had a good year, but second best is not good enough."

Clearly it wasn't. While the Bears allowed 28 points in their opener, which they won by 10, it was clear to see this compilation of great talent, led by the incomparable Walter Payton, was not to be stopped. While Ditka was the fiery head coach, Buddy Ryan was the defensive coordinator, and they didn't get along very well because, well, they both had giant egos.

"To this day, Mike will say, 'Let's face it, we wouldn't have been in the Super Bowl if we didn't have Buddy Ryan.' What happened chronologically was, I had written a letter and covered my butt, having all of the defensive players sign it, to George Halas [then the owner of the Bears]. We knew our coaching staff was going to get fired, and I think Alan Page, who was retiring that year, said if we don't do something, they're going to get rid of this entire coaching staff."

Fencik was very reluctant about writing the letter to Halas, but eventually he did, and that changed everything.

"George Halas showed up during practice. He had never been to a practice, and we were practicing indoors at the Great Lakes Naval Training Center. And I knew right away it was the letter I had written. And he told our coaches—and I'll never forget this—he told our coaches to take a hike! He said, 'I got that letter. I've never gotten a letter like that,' and said, 'Your [defensive] coaches will be back next year.' I knew when Neill Armstrong and his coaching staff got fired after the 1981 season, I'm sure Buddy wanted the head coaching job, but Ditka was hired as the head coach."

It was an almost a surreal press conference with dozens of microphones and a full house of reporters watching the crusty Halas installing his great tight end from the 1963 championship team as head coach.

"But Ditka had to inherit the defensive coordinator Buddy Ryan. I just think in any organization, that's difficult, and it worked. There was this dynamic tension that was unbelievable. But at the end of the day, Buddy got a head coaching job [with the Philadelphia Eagles in 1986], which was best for him. And that was the end of the road, if you will. And even though Vince Tobin ran a lot of things based on what Buddy did, he had his own style. We had great stats in '86, and the defense—hey, it wasn't just Buddy Ryan—we were a pretty good group, as well, and we're going to show everybody."

The Bears were still a prominent team. They went 14-2 in 1986 but lost in the first round of the playoffs. Then the players' strike two weeks into the 1987 season cast a pall on that season. They went 11-4 in 1987 but again lost in the first round of the playoffs. The 1988 team went 12-4 but lost in the NFC Championship Game. A couple more winning seasons followed in 1990 and 1991, but no more Super Bowls for a team that appeared as if it might win two or three! The Bears went 5-11 in 1992, and Ditka was fired.

The 1985 team's only loss was at Miami to the Dolphins, which remains the only team to go through a full season including play-offs, undefeated.

# Dave Wannstedt

FIND ME a better storyteller than this guy! Dave Wannstedt can weave a yarn with the very best of them. Not only are his stories interesting, they're amusing if not downright hilarious. The man has a gift few of us have. Wake him up in the middle of the night, and I guarantee you he'll tell you a humorous story. Wannstedt is the former head coach of the Chicago Bears and Miami Dolphins, as well as the University of Pittsburgh. But how appropriate is it that he morphed into a commentator, where his stories flow like a river? Wannstedt currently works as a studio host on Fox Sports, along with roles on Chicago radio and TV.

Wannstedt's coaching career spanned 38 years, from a grad assistant at Pitt to his last job as a special-teams coach for the Tampa Bay Buccaneers. A native of Pennsylvania, which has a reputation for churning out football coaches, Wannstedt was also a late-round draft pick by the Green Bay Packers. But he spent the year on injured reserve and never played a down in the NFL. He did manage to carve out a solid coaching career, although his six-year tenure with the Bears resulted in only one playoff appearance. He did make consecutive playoff appearances with the Dolphins after replacing Jimmy Johnson as head coach, but it was downhill after that. Wannstedt tells many stories about Johnson, whom he also coached under with the Dallas Cowboys. And he probably tells more about then fellow assistant Tony Wise, who joined Wannstedt's staff in Chicago. The two remain the dearest of friends. If there's ever an award for most valuable storyteller, "Wanny" would win it every year.

My first association with Wanny occurred in the early 1990s, when I covered Bears training camp in Platteville, Wisconsin. He had replaced the iconic Mike Ditka as head coach. It might have been a tough act to follow, but the Bears went 5–11 in Ditka's final season. Wanny went 7–9 in his first season then posted back-to-back 9–7 campaigns, making the playoffs in 1994. For a guy who was talkative as a kid—he said that's the way people from Pittsburgh are—he would tell the media stories that always left us laughing. And it was how he delivered them, with his Pennsylvania drawl, that made them even more enticing. It's interesting to note that, when Wanny starting coaching the Bears, his opinion of talk radio wasn't exactly a glowing one.

"Somebody asked me in a press conference what I thought of talk radio," he recalled, "and my comment was, 'Anybody who would call in and listen to that stuff are the same people who think that studio wrestling is for real!'"

Now Wannstedt is doing *two* 670 The Score radio shows twice a week in drive time and sometimes more! What Wannstedt realized after he was done coaching was that he didn't have to be as guarded as to what he could say. Thus a new career in the media.

Perhaps the best of the many stories Wannstedt told me during our podcast was when the Bears decided to hire him. It began with the Bears' then PR director Bryan Harlan not meeting Wannstedt until the day he was given the job.

"I didn't find that out until the day he and I shook hands, and he kind of looked at me with a look... 'Oh, good to see you. Glad you're here. Excuse me for 10 minutes while I go in my office and [look up] your history so I can give you something to talk about at the press conference.'"

Of course, I'm laughing, but this is just the beginning of a story that goes back a few days.

"I accepted the Bears job while I was still the assistant head coach with the Dallas Cowboys, and it was during the bye week before the Super Bowl. [The NFL has since changed the rule about when a coach can take another job in the league.]... I fly to Chicago and accept the job the day we beat the 49ers for the right to go to the Super Bowl."

This is where the story gets intriguing.

"All I got from Mike McCaskey [the late president of the Bears] and his secretary was, this is where you're staying. The driver will take you to the Deer Path Inn in Lake Forest, and you're to check in under the name George Trafton. Now I'm thinking to myself, *George Trafton*? I look him up, and he's the first Bear to play center in the 1920s. First center that has the reputation of snapping the ball with one hand. That's what he's known for. Great player, Hall of Fame player. So I'm saying to my wife, 'Wow! This is really secrecy here.'"

"Secrecy" is one way of putting it.

"I'm going to see Mike McCaskey the next day, so this is, check in to your hotel, check in under a false name, go to your room, and someone will pick you up in the morning. I'm gonna go along with it, okay!"

Little did Wannstedt realize what was about to happen.

"My wife and I get out of the car, and I don't even get to the front door of the Deer Path Inn, and the doorman opens the door, and he says, 'Coach! Welcome to Chicago.'"

At this point, I'm laughing so hard I need oxygen.

"I walk in the lobby, and the guy there says, 'Can I take your bag, Coach?' Now I have to go up to the front desk and tell this poor girl I'm George Trafton! She looks at me. So I sign in as George Trafton, and I said to my wife, 'This is ridiculous. I need a drink!' I turned to the guy and said, 'Do you have a lounge or restaurant where I can get something to eat and a beer?' So we sat down in a booth, and I remember this like it was yesterday, the waiter comes up to us and says, 'Hey, Coach, welcome to Chicago.' It was no secret, everybody in the hotel knew who we were and what we're doing. I think my picture was on the front page of the paper. Somebody sent me a picture of the *Chicago Tribune*, and it says, 'He's the Guy,' and I'm standing there on the sideline of the Super Bowl in Dallas Cowboy gear! So, yes, they knew. Heck yeah, who didn't? Oh, wow, it was a classic."

Welcome to the Chicago Bears, Coach. If you think this is ridiculous and a classic, consider what happened after Wannstedt was fired in 1998. The Bears had interviewed Dave McGinnis, a former linebackers coach for 10 seasons, and it looked like they were going to hire him. They even called a press conference for him the next day, only there was one very large wrinkle: he had not yet received a formal offer or contract details. Meanwhile, ex-players were calling to congratulate him, while the media assembled for the 11:00 AM press conference McGinnis knew nothing about. McGinnis met McCaskey in his office, as the media waited. The press conference was delayed, as McCaskey then made a contract offer not to McGinnis's liking. The press conference was called off. The two sides met the next day, but much to the chagrin of McGinnis, who had wanted the job, and the Bears, who were thoroughly embarrassed by the situation, McGinnis bolted for Phoenix, where he returned as the Arizona Cardinals' defensive coordinator.

So it wasn't the first time and, considering the Bears, it might not be the last time.

And it won't be the last time you hear a story, and probably a very funny one, from Wanny.

# Dan Hampton

DANIMAL! If you reside in and around the Chicago area or even if you don't and happen to be a football fan, the nickname is synonymous with one person: Dan Hampton. The Hall of Fame defensive lineman was part of Chicago's only Super Bowl–winning team, the 1985 Bears. That defensive unit was considered by many to be the greatest of all time. The Bears went a combined 18-1, including the postseason, and only five times did they give up more than 10 points. Hampton was a linchpin, having been the fourth pick in the first round of the 1979 NFL Draft. Armed with strength, size, and a menacing disposition, Hampton played all 12 of his seasons in Chicago, but he also accumulated myriad injuries. He had 10 knee surgeries during that time. He had several more after retirement.

It didn't take Hampton long to find his second career in the media. He is a cohost of *Pro Football Weekly* and has been an analyst on WGN radio. He's also charity-driven, being part of "Gridiron Greats," which raises funds for retired NFL players in need, and he's also part of "One for the Kids," an annual golf tournament held for children.

But there's also been a darker side to Hampton. He's received four DUIs, including one in his native Arkansas that landed him in jail for a week!

Danimal was fun to interview, just as he was while I was covering those great Bears teams of the 1980s. He was engaging and never at a loss for words, which explains why he's had a successful life as a broadcaster. He is fiercely loyal, deciding he wanted his graphic for my podcast to be with his arms around a frail Steve McMichael, his former teammate who is battling ALS (Lou Gehrig's Disease).

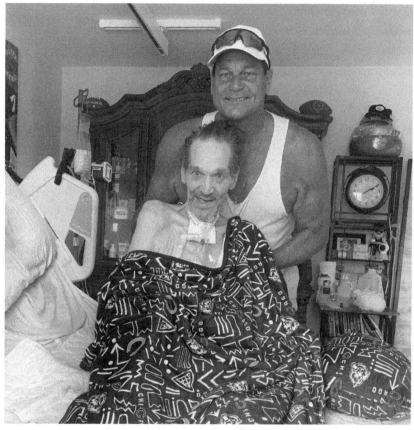

*Dan Hampton with Steve McMichael* (Photograph courtesy of Dan Hampton)

During our interview, Danimal discussed his unique and popular nickname; the iconic Walter Payton, for whom he delivered two riveting speeches for entirely different reasons; and the founder of the Bears and a co-founder of the NFL, George Halas.

"I think it was 1982. It was Ditka's first year and a strike-shortened year. I was playing pretty well, and I remember we were down in Tampa Bay, and we're kicking their ass pretty good. Pat Summerall and John Madden were doing the game, and the week prior they had done a Dallas Cowboys game. My buddy, Randy White [then with the Cowboys], we were buddies in the Pro Bowl, and we both played defensive tackle and both in the NFC. Randy had a nickname called the "Manster," and Madden, in the fourth quarter said, 'Randy White is the Manster so this guy Hampton is the Danimal.'"

Hindsight is 20-20, but Hampton figured he could have made millions.

"I wished I would have went and trademarked that nickname because, guess what? Some company has the nickname for one of its products, and it's a multimillion-dollar product."

The company happens to be Dannon, which uses "Danimals" for a brand of its low-fat drinkable yogurt that it launched in 1994.

"That's unbelievable! And you know what? They say football players are smart guys."

As Hampton chuckled, I remembered how so many other players on those Bears teams of the 1980s had great nicknames. There was "Sweetness" for Walter Payton, "Mongo" for Steve McMichael, "Samurai Mike" for Mike Singletary, and "the Punky QB" for Jim McMahon.

"It was the 100th anniversary of the NFL, and we were named the greatest team of all time!"

As I mentioned earlier, Hampton had a close relationship with Walter Payton, who died in 1999 as a result of cancer caused by a rare liver disease. Hampton was one of those who was called upon to give a eulogy at Soldier Field during a public memorial honoring the Hall of Fame running back.

"Honestly, and in a strange way, I kind of feel a part of destiny here in the sense that, I got to meet him in 1979. I played nine years with him. Obviously, we know the complications he had with bile duct cancer. It took his life on November 1, 1999.

"So it's 1-1-1-1-9-9-9. I remember at the time Brian McCaskey [one of the sons of Bears owner Virginia McCaskey], my dear friend, called me and said, 'They're going to do a memorial for Walter at Soldier Field, and we'd like to have some people speak.'"

It didn't take an emotional Hampton long to say he just couldn't do it. But McCaskey responded by saying, "Who will?"

"So anyway, I said, 'I'll be there.'"

This is part of what Hampton said at the memorial:

> I got a little girl, she's four years old. Ten years from now
> when she asks me about the Chicago Bears, I'll tell her about
> a championship and great teams and great teammates and
> great coaches and how great it was to be a part of it.

But then, in a halting and emotional voice Hampton continued:

> But the first thing I would tell her about is Walter Payton!

The crowd cheered.

Twenty years later, Hampton was there for the dedication of
the statue of Payton outside Soldier Field. Here's some of what he
said:

> After winning six championships with the Chicago Bears,
> George Halas and Jim Finks [then the team's general man-
> ager] decided on drafting a young man who would become
> the heart and soul of Halas's final championship team. That
> was Walter Payton.

The timing of the statue was perfect.

"That was great. The 100-year anniversary of the Chicago
Bears—they commemorated it with a statue of George Halas and
Walter Payton, the founder and the greatest player."

Hampton's relationship with Payton was joyful, and he knew
when he got here in 1979 how big Payton had already become.
"When I got to Chicago, I didn't know a whole lot about it, but I was
eager to learn what's going on. So, when I got here, Walter Payton
was the story. He was like a movie star, like *Miami Vice*. He had the
Jheri curl and sunglasses, the Lamborghini. He was a movie star,
and it was great to meet him and great to be a part of his world. You
have no idea how tough his career path was."

The Bears were just building these great teams, and Payton was their main weapon. Their major pieces would come in subsequent years, including Mike Ditka, who was named head coach in 1982.

"I'll never forget the night before the Super Bowl, Ditka said, "I'm basically done. All year long, I have been motivating you. I want the captains to stand up and say what this game means." Walter got up and had tears in his eyes. He was in his 11th year and said, 'I've accomplished a lot, but I've always wanted to be a winner. If we win the Super Bowl tomorrow, we'll be the greatest team on planet Earth. And I can put my head on the pillow and say, at long last, 'I'm a winner.' That really struck a chord with all of us."

Hampton admitted it was hard to sleep the night before the Super Bowl. He was ready to suit up the night before the game. The Bears overwhelmed the Patriots 46-10, but Payton didn't score a touchdown, something Ditka regrets to this very day.

# Dave Eanet

THE FIRST thing you think of when you hear the name Dave Eanet is Northwestern. He's been the voice of Wildcats football since 1990 and basketball since 1996. Eanet is as synonymous with Northwestern athletics as anyone, and "Mr. Cat," as he's known, had the broadcast booth at Ryan Field named after him in 2014. Northwestern has produced some very famous people in the broadcast industry, including Mike Greenberg, Michael Wilbon, Brent Musburger, Rich Eisen, Mike Adamle, Ron Gleason (who retired as the director of news and programming at WBBM Newsradio in early 2023), and several others. But it's Eanet who stands alone for his longtime service to the university.

A native of Washington, D.C., Eanet began his career at WBBM as a student, where he was a newswriter. But since sports was his biggest interest, he befriended Brad Palmer and Rich King, two very prominent members of the Chicago sports media for decades. In 1983 Eanet returned to Washington, only to come back to Chicago a year later to join WGN radio. Three years after that, it was back to WBBM, where his career with Northwestern would start before yet another move back to WGN. He's been there ever since, doing morning drive sports along with his role with Northwestern.

I got to know "the Great Dave Eanet" early on, as we both covered games. The nickname is well deserved for me personally. I was employed at Chicago Sports Webio in 2009. It was an Internet sports venue and ceased to exist after just nine weeks of operation after it was revealed it was run through a Ponzi scheme. I turned to to Dave and asked if he had anything available at WGN. He said no, but a month later he called back and told me there was some part-time work he could give me. I was thrilled, to say the least, but there was an issue. I had what I thought was laryngitis and told Dave I should be ready in about 10 days. That was late July. But a subsequent discovery was made: I had a paralyzed vocal cord. I could barely talk. I was treated for it for some four months until finally, in early November, I had a gel injected into my neck so I could get my voice back. And guess what? The job at WGN was still there, and Eanet hired me. I was on the air four days later and worked there until late August 2010 when I hooked on at WBBM. I can never thank Dave enough for saving my career.

There are two stories I would like to share with you from the interview. The first involves the Bears' trip to New Orleans and Super Bowl XX on January 26, 1986.

"That date is close to the heart of a lot of people, Super Bowl XX," Dave said. "I was at the time working with the Bears radio crew. I produced the games in the booth and did some pregame and halftime work on air. I produced the broadcast with Wayne Larrivee, Jim Hart, and Dick Butkus on WGN and did the postgame show with Chuck Swirsky."

But Eanet had yet another role, accompany Butkus to record his pregame interview with Bears head coach Mike Ditka.

"Normally we did that at the stadium, but seeing how it was the Super Bowl, we figured maybe we ought to do it ahead of time. It was decided we would go to Ditka's suite in the team hotel. So we go into his suite, which was a very large suite as I remember, and we go in, and what I remember about it was Ditka was very calm outwardly—I don't know what he was like on the inside—but I got the feeling everyone kind of knew what was going to happen."

And everyone was right. The Bears routed the New England Patriots 46–10!

"We get done with the interview, and it's a couple of hours before gametime, so Dick and I decide we're just going to walk over to the Superdome."

Little did they realize what was about to happen, at least not Eanet.

"I'm walking alongside Dick Butkus. Now, keep in mind, Dick Butkus would be recognized in, I don't know, Laramie, Wyoming.

But on this particular day in New Orleans, everybody who was driving by or was stopped in traffic that was gridlocked realized that was Dick Butkus, one of the greatest Bears of all time. And they're all stopping and leaning out of their cars and yelling to Dick, 'Go get 'em, Butkus!'"

Butkus had a great reaction to all of this. He was used to the adulation and fame that went his way, and not long after would start appearing in movies.

"He was savoring every minute of this, because I think he was excited as anybody the Bears were in the Super Bowl, but about to win the Super Bowl! It was the coolest reaction, watching Dick react to the fans and savoring this very important moment in Chicago history."

Another memory Eanet had was vastly different than the first one but a part of history, as well. When Eanet was eight years old, he endured what many of us did, the assassination of President John F. Kennedy on November 22, 1963. It had a profound effect on so many of us, including the young Eanet.

"I was in third grade, and we had the day off from school that day. It was a cool, cloudy Friday. My friends and I were playing in this wooded area around their house, and it's around the middle of the day, and one of my friends' older brothers comes running out and says the president has been assassinated."

I was nearly 10, but Eanet echoed what I felt: neither of us quite understood what *assassinated* meant. I remember when I heard he was shot, telling others he'd be okay. Eanet surmised *assassinated* wasn't a very encouraging word.

"It shows you how things were so different back then. So what do you do? We ran to the local drugstore, and everyone's huddled around, of course, a black-and-white TV watching the news coverage. I lived about a block and a half from there. We all scattered, and I ran home. I run upstairs and my mom and sister have the TV on."

Eanet's mother was crying, and it was the first time he had ever seen her cry. Eanet remembers that, when the networks weren't showing news coverage, they went to this funereal music and black-and-white graphics.

"As an eight-year-old, that stuff hits you harder than the actual event because I didn't fully understand what had just gone on. That Sunday, they were taking the president's body to the Capitol with a procession down Pennsylvania Avenue."

It's a scene that is indelibly etched in my memory.

"A friend of mine and his father asked me if I wanted to go with them to see it. So it's freezing cold, and we go down there, and what I remember is the caisson with the flag-draped casket and the riderless horse. Those are the things that kind of stay with you."

I certainly can echo that. I was glued to the television for three days!

"They took the casket to the Capitol Rotunda. We stood in line, and we were going to see the president lying in state. I didn't know what the term meant. We're not in a state, we're in the District of Columbia! That's what we were taught in school. But we stood in line for what seemed like hours, but it probably wasn't because it was absolutely freezing, and my friend's dad, realizing he had two eight-year-old kids whose teeth were chattering and whose hands were turning blue, decided we weren't going to get in for five or six hours and took us home."

It's funny the things you remember from your childhood. Those images have stayed with Eanet and many others who witnessed this life-changing event.

# Ron Rivera

HE'S KNOWN as "Riverboat Ron," but around the Chicagoland area he will always be known as "Chico." Ron Rivera, head coach of the Washington Commanders, was a member of the Chicago Bears Super Bowl champs in 1985. He spent nine seasons with them as a linebacker on one of the most ferocious defenses in NFL history. An army brat whose father was stationed in Germany, Panama, and then Washington, D.C., the personable Rivera became a football star in his new home in Marina, California. He attended the University of California–Berkeley, and while playing for the Golden Bears was named Pac-10 Defensive Player of the Year in 1983. It's one of the reasons the Bears chose him in the second round of the 1984 draft. Rivera flourished under head coach Mike Ditka. Five years after he retired, Rivera began his new career: coaching as the Bears' quality control coach. After taking a job as linebackers coach with the Philadelphia Eagles, Rivera was named the Bears' defensive coordinator in 2004. But he left after three seasons and a Super Bowl appearance, as he didn't see eye to eye with then head coach Lovie Smith. But in 2011, Rivera was named head coach of the Carolina Panthers, where he would make a name for himself. He was twice named NFL Coach of the Year (in 2013 and 2015) and took his Panthers to Super Bowl 50, where they lost to the Denver Broncos. Rivera spent nine years in Carolina and, in 2020, was named head coach of the Washington franchise.

Chico was one of those guys who had a favorable relationship with the media. Whether it was as a player or coach, he was always accessible and friendly, as if he were your neighbor. Remember, he was part of a Bears team that had a spate of personalities, but Chico was a little more low-key than some of the others. Surprisingly, he was not part of the "Super Bowl Shuffle," the song performed by more than 20 members of the team and that remarkably hit No. 41 on the Billboard charts. Chico claimed it was too early in the morning after the Bears lost their only game of the 1985 season in a Monday night game at Miami. He has no regrets. But you could see Chico had leadership qualities. He was upfront and straightforward during interviews but always injected a sense of boldness. It's always been part of his makeup.

Chico was a wonderful interview, taking me down memory lane, along with telling delightful and funny stories. Here are two. The first one is how Rivera got his nickname, Chico.

"When I got to the Bears, Buddy Ryan was still the defensive coordinator. And Buddy took a shine to me, and one of the things Buddy had a tendency of doing, he would give you a nickname, and that was who you were. Buddy would either call you by your jersey number or your nickname. Well, one of Buddy's favorite TV shows was *Chico and the Man.* He thought I looked a little like Freddie Prinze [who played Chico]. So he nicknamed me Chico. What was kind of funny and apropos about it was, during practice, Buddy would have me stand next to him about 25 or 30 yards behind the defense."

Ryan would signal defenses in and call plays from back there, and he would ask Rivera questions. "'Why do you think we're doing this?' and 'What do you expect out of that formation?' 'When they shift and line up like this, what are you anticipating?' He was basically teaching me and grilling me on what to expect and whether I was paying attention and learning. It was my formal education as a football player, and little did I know it was going to be my formal education as I was learning to become a defensive coordinator."

Now you know how and why Rivera became a coach. Another story Rivera told was about his relationship with teammate and Hall of Famer Dan Hampton. This was also a kind of formal education, only for a very different reason.

"One of my favorite stories always revolves around Dan Hampton. He was truly one of the all-time greats and should be remembered as that. During training camp, Hamp had this disdain for curfew. So one of things he used to do was sneak out. Coach

Ditka and my room were next to the back door at the dorms in Platteville, Wisconsin."

This where the Bears trained for 18 years. I remember it well, albeit by the rather unpleasant odor that hit me as I neared town. The fields were awash in fertilizer. Enough said.

"So whenever 'Hoss' would come home late at night, it would be my room he would toss rocks up against the glass, and that would wake me. I would run to the glass and loom out, and here was Hamp pointing at the back door. So I would have to go downstairs to the back door and let him in. What would happen is, every now and then he would do it three nights in row. And the problem with that is, Hamp never practiced in the morning. He would always practice in the afternoon. So, if he missed curfew, it wasn't much of a big deal."

This started to become a concern for Rivera. Actually, it became an annoyance.

"But waking me up three nights in a row at 2:00 o'clock in the morning was a little too much. So one day I say, 'Hoss, enough is enough. Forget it, you've got to stop! You're killing me, because I have to practice in the morning and you don't.' He said, 'All right, Chico, we're good, don't worry about it.'"

You're probably ahead of yourself thinking about the resulting scenario.

"So, lo and behold, the next night, guess what happens? I hear that ting of rock up against my window. I open up, and there's Hamp. He points at the door, and I wave and I close the drape and I don't go down and open the door. I lay back down."

Let's face it: if anything, Hampton was persistent.

"So, a couple minutes later, I hear another ting against the glass, and I open the glass up and I wave my finger, no, no, no! I closed the drapes, turned off the lights, and lay back down. All of a sudden, he throws his flip-flop up against my window. So I heard the big slap this time, and I opened up the drapes and I looked down and flip him the bird! Closed the drape, turned the light off and all of a sudden he threw a brick through my window!"

I responded with, "I had a feeling that was coming." Didn't you? We both laughed.

"I run downstairs, and I'm really pissed at him, and I said, 'Listen, Hoss, that's it man. I'm gonna tell you right now, and when they ask me how I broke my window, I'm gonna say Dan Hampton threw a rock through my window trying to wake me up at 2:00 o'clock in the morning because he had broken curfew.' He said, 'No, Chico, calm down.' I said, 'No, no, Hoss, that's too much.' I said, 'Look, dude, give me the check.'"

Rivera made Hampton give him the weekly check they would get for training camp.

"It's like a thousand dollars. So he signed over his check to me, and to this day I've never told Coach Ditka."

Maybe it's time to tell Ditka. Better yet, maybe he'll read about it right here!

# Laura Okmin

IF YOU'RE a fan of the National Football League and don't know who Laura Okmin is, perhaps you should switch to badminton. Okmin is the third-longest-tenured sideline reporter in league history. She's been patrolling the sidelines for more than 200 games, including a number of Super Bowls. But her credits go far beyond being a sideline reporter. Okmin has been a host/anchor and reporter for the summer and winter Olympic games and national college games. She also created a 30-minute series about NFL players off the field. But going back even further, she worked as a host for CNN's sports programming and, in the mid-1990s, worked in Chicago, where her duties included live postgame interviews during the Bulls' playoff runs, which meant rubbing shoulders with one Michael Jordan.

That said, Okmin's biggest contribution might be her company, GALvanize, which helps train and mentor young women entering the business of sports and broadcasting. GALvanize has amassed more than 2,500, women, and it's growing with each passing day.

I was fortunate to meet Laura on the beat, and she was thrilled to be back in Chicago, since she was brought up here. She was filled with enthusiasm but also focused on getting better every day, and Chicago is a major sports market with a competitive media. When Laura arrived, she was supposed to focus on the Bears beat, and her first partner was the legendary Doug Buffone, the lovable and iconic ex-Bear who then became a memorable star on sports radio. But her focus then turned to an even more iconic figure, perhaps the most iconic in U.S. sports history, Michael Jordan. Laura traveled with Jordan and the Bulls on their run to a second threepeat. Laura grew exponentially better as a professional during that time, but maintained that, whenever she was rushed to do any interview, she had to say hello to her subject first.

"I know as a young reporter I floundered," she admitted. "I was so young and naïve. I thought I was ready, and I wasn't in so many ways. I wasn't ready as a journalist, I wasn't ready in press conferences, when people looked at [me] when I asked a question. I struggled confidence-wise. And I struggled, learning how to build relationships as a woman, when there weren't very many of us."

Funny thing, though, it appears Okmin was already thinking ahead about ways to help others.

"I got to an age where I needed women in my life. I needed women who had gone through it or were going through it. The best friend I had in the business was a man. He helped me up to a point, but couldn't understand what it was like as a woman. I saw woman get thrown in quicker than I did and higher up than I did."

The biggest issue for Okmin was the women who weren't ready, and she saw networks chew them up and spit them out. These were women who were in their early twenties, and Okmin watched as some of them had their confidence crushed. Her fortune was she saw this at an older age, when she could do something about it.

"Instead of getting judgmental, I got more protective."

That was some 14 years ago.

"It took me about four months to find 20 women who wanted to get into a conference room and spend a weekend talking about women in sports. I didn't think of it as a business or a title, I just wanted to help!"

As GALvanize has grown, it's not just women on camera, it's women all the way from high school right into their forties!

"It's been an incredible sisterhood of women to help build and help be a part of because it's something I never would have had. Now I'm glad I didn't have it because I wouldn't have created it. We're all ages, though the sweet spot is between 23 and 27, so that's probably the bulk. When they come to me, they're just starting, and to be able to help and hopefully give a springboard and this great sisterhood to help them. I've seen every one of them follow their dreams. Whether it's on camera or producing or PR or an agent, I've also seen GALvanize change their path."

What Okmin aimed for was women to see a bigger world. In other words, not just being on camera. GALvanize also partners up with other professional sports leagues so these women can see player engagement. The idea is also to expand roles to sales and operations.

By virtue of GALvanize, Okmin has become a trailblazer of a different sort.

"This business is really selfish. It's so much about you, it's so much about my path, what job do I want? What network do I want to aspire to work for? What event do I want to cover? I got to an age where I was fortunate I checked a lot of boxes, and had a very sad life with those checked boxes and said, what else is there? I had so much passion for my career and still do, but I had no purpose. I was kind of sleepwalking, event to event, airplane to airplane. So I hope what GALvanize did was give me the purpose to go along with the passion."

Although Okmin doesn't have any children, she now likes to think that, with GALvanize, she has more than 2,500 of them.

"It just opened my heart and grew my heart in ways I didn't know it could grow. Now I love when I get a great assignment, I love when I have a great interview, but my heart grows 10 times bigger when one of my women does. I hope I created something that wasn't there when I started in the business that will last a whole lot longer than my career will."

But when I suggested women have come a long way, Okmin said she was torn with this notion.

"Yes, there are women doing things that you and I probably never thought. I was asked 20 years ago, will a woman be in a booth calling play-by-play or coach, and I would say not in my lifetime. We have, in terms of that, but what I always say is, we've come a long way in numbers but not in a meaningful or sustainable way. For me to feel women have come far in this business means we really need to see women running the rooms. We need to see women creating and owning the content. We need to see women hiring. We need to see women in the executive rooms and boardrooms. I'd say we have come far in numbers, but we have such a far way to go in terms of creating something that will allow us to name just one woman as a coach or three as play-by-play. I think to say we've come a long way, baby, is finally when we're in those high offices and making major decisions as to who we're hiring and what content we're creating. When that happens, then, yes, we've finally come a far way!"

It's interesting to note that the most prominent role women in sports fill today is sideline reporting, and it's in most of the major sports. Okmin says she prepares just as hard as the play-by-play announcer and analyst, but they might get three-plus hours and she might get two-plus minutes! This is not to say Okmin is dissatisfied with her role. On the contrary.

"There has to be more women in bigger roles that it's not just literally and figuratively on the sideline."

Sarah Kustok, Lisa Byington, and Cheryl Raye-Stout have also been guests on my podcast. And, like Okmin, all are trailblazers. Kustok became the first female analyst for an NBA team (New Jersey); Byington became the first lead announcer (Milwaukee); and Raye-Stout is a radio producer and reporter in Chicago. The list is growing.

So far, Okmin is living out two dreams. Her success and that of her company, GALvanize.

# Jeff Joniak

HE IS the ebullient voice of the Chicago Bears. Entering his 23rd season behind the mic and now with a new radio station, WMVP–ESPN 1000, Joniak is just as excited as he was when he first took the job in 2001. He had previously worked as the pregame host and reporter. He had never called a football game before but provided the station with a résumé produced from calling games into a tape reporter. But to obtain the job, Joniak also had to agree to do afternoon sports anchoring at WBBM Newsradio, then the home of the Bears. And he had to do that while reporting from Halas Hall, the Bears in-season practice site. After convincing management, Joniak also had to do the same to an audience of knowledgeable Bears fans. It took a while, but he along with analyst Tom Thayer, a member of the 1985 Super Bowl champs, managed to win over a legion of listeners. Previous voices of the Bears include Wayne Larrivee, now the voice of the rival Green Bay Packers; Joe McConnell, the crisp and fast-talking announcer; and the legendary Jack Brickhouse, who had the longest run at 24 years.

Joniak's job as voice of the Bears includes the team's many speaking engagements and his weekly postgame TV appearance with Lou Canellis.

Joniak is a graduate of Hersey High School in Arlington Heights. He began his career at SportsPhone, where I began mine. He also worked at the Illinois News Network, CLTV, and on Bulls broadcasts. He has won numerous awards for his work.

I've known J.J. for more than 35 years, but it took some 25 before he became my boss at WBBM, from 2010 to 2020. Prior to that, I constantly engaged with J.J., both in person, covering events, and on the phone, where we would discuss the sports stories and issues of the day. I really enjoyed those conversations because J.J.

is so opinionated. He can be effusive and demanding. He doesn't hold back, which is an admirable trait. He'll let you know when he doesn't like something, but then compliment you on your work.

J.J.'s climb to success has come through an obsession with hard work and determination. He doesn't cut corners—witness the countless hours he spends covering the Bears.

And J.J. loves to kid. He would make up stories, and his foil would always be the late and beloved Eric Brown, a longtime sports reporter for WBBM before he died from colon cancer in 2014. He tried this with me but would fail miserably!

Every play-by-play announcer has a home run, hockey goal, or touchdown call. J.J.'s is "Touchdown, touchdown Bears." But J.J. developed another call, which today remains one of the most renowned nationwide, and it was attached to one of the most successful and dramatic kickoff and punt returners in NFL history.

*"Devin Hester...you are ridiculous!"*

"It was never planned," Joniak said, "but I use that word repeatedly, because that's my stock answer, and I usually pair it with a no-no word."

This is understandable, because if you witnessed some of Hester's returns, you too might have been prompted to utter an invective or two.

"I think it caught me so off guard," he recalled. "It was in St. Louis in 2006, his rookie year, a Super Bowl year for the Bears. I believe it was the second return touchdown of that game. I knew it was going to happen. That's why it shook me and had me have an out-of-body experience. It's hard not to be a fan calling games, but you can't be, otherwise you're going to miss a lot."

But it's also not hard to forget such a ground-breaking moment because it changed the way special-teams started covering kickoffs and punt returns.

"I just remember the gap between where he caught the ball and the nearest defender, and I'm like, ring it up!"

The excitement in Joniak's voice as he described the play was palpable.

"And in my mind, I'm already building up. It took just a matter of seconds for him to get in the end zone, and I just let loose because it was the second one.

*Devin Hester...you are ridiculous!*

"How many times are teams going to kick to him? And I think it was just exuberance and a stunning reality that this guy is unique and special. I remember the ceiling in the broadcast booth in the old RCA Dome, Tom [Thayer] would hit his head on the ceiling. And the television's hung low, but I glanced up to see [then head coach] Lovie Smith's reaction, and I used it on the air. Lovie Smith's jaw just literally dropped, because that's what it was! He was in stunned amazement."

As for the use of the phrase, "Devin Hester, you are ridiculous," Joniak said he didn't really think much of it until he got on the team bus after the game.

"The first person I see is Mike Mulligan [then a beat writer for the *Chicago Tribune* and now morning host on 670 the Score]. He says, 'Your call, your call your call.' I go, 'What call?' And he says, 'Don't be that way, it's all over the place.' And I'm like, 'The Hester one?'"

Little did Joniak realize he just created a monster, and a long-lasting one.

"And the next morning, the world changed for me, honestly. Everybody stopped me on the street. I'll go to a bar these days, and these guys want to buy you a shot if you say, 'You are ridiculous.' I just think it's hilarious because it's an unintended reality."

Interestingly enough, this was not the first term Joniak used to describe a Hester touchdown.

"That year I used something I did come up with. That was the opener against Green Bay, and he returned a kickoff for a touchdown, and I called him the 'Windy City Flyer.' That was a pretty good nickname [for a guy] who ran a 4.2 40-yard dash. He had moves like I'd never seen since Gale Sayers."

Sayers, the Hall of Fame running back, had a combined eight returns for touchdowns, but his career kick-return average was 30.6

yards, still an NFL record. A knee injury limited his career to just seven seasons. Hester holds the NFL record for touchdowns on special teams with 20—14 of them on kickoff returns, five on punt returns, and one on a missed field goal. He also holds the single-season record for most returns for a touchdown with six in 2007.

Joniak remembered a time he was at a Bears convention a couple of year after Hester's emergence: "I stopped and literally went into emcee mode, because there was a guy in the front row wearing a shirt that says WINDY CITY FLYER with the Chicago skyline. Now, for years, people told me you had to monetize your call. I never once thought about that. I'm not the world's greatest capitalist. So I stopped and said, 'Hey, buddy, where did you get that shirt?' And the guy replies, 'I got it at Walgreens'! I was so ticked off. But Devin told me when he was living in Chicago he had a mural painted on his wall with the Chicago skyline and WINDY CITY FLYER on it. I thought that was pretty cool."

We then got into the subject of Hester's contribution to the game and the fact that he belongs in the Pro Football Hall of Fame.

"That's 100 percent accurate," Joniak said. "I've said it a million times. He single-handedly changed the way teams build their special-teams units—both punt and kickoff returns. Seriously, they had to deal with this guy, and you know what, everybody stopped kicking to him. I remember once in a Denver game, Todd Sauerbrun, former Bears punter, mis-hit a punt, and Hester leaped over him in the open field and finished the job. And every player who blocked for him couldn't wait to get out there. Everybody got off the bench and wanted to watch him go to work."

The same could be said of the fans who got off their seats and screamed in delight when Hester would run back a kick.

And then there was the Super Bowl—Super Bowl XLI, which started off with a bang!

"What little kid grows up thinking he's going to call a Super Bowl? Not this one. And I'm there. I remember being a nervous wreck and walking into the stands to see my uncle. My dad died young, so he was like a dad to me, and I just start bawling. He had never seen this before, and he had tears in his eyes, and I'm an emotional wreck. So, opening kickoff, all I want to say is, flashbulbs popping at Miami. Never once did I think Hester would take the opening kickoff—never done in Super Bowl history—for a touchdown. And soon as he made a patented cut in the middle of the field, I said, 'Oh My God!' One half of my brain is thinking, 'This is gonna go, you gotta capture this moment, it's the Super Bowl.' And the other, 'You're describing it.'"

And Joniak did in pulsating fashion, but there was a fear factor attached.

"I swear it was a slow-motion, out-of-body experience. I let it rip and blew out my voice. It took me one year to listen to that broadcast because I was so fearful I didn't give it its due. I was afraid to listen to it."

*Jeff Joniak....you are ridiculous!*

# Tom Thayer

THERE ARE not many members of the Super Bowl–champion 1985 Bears who remain as prominent as Tom Thayer. He's been a radio analyst on Bears broadcasts since 1997, and before that hosted the *Tom and Keith Show* on WLUP—with Keith Van Horne, who also played on the '85 Bears. Basically, Thayer has been part of the Bears since he joined the team during that fabled 1985 season. His enduring voice has been a comfort for Bears fans, like a favorite pillow. He's passionate, knowledgeable, and very easy to listen to.

But this native of Joliet, Illinois, was also a star player at Joliet Catholic High School and then at Notre Dame, where he was named an honorable mention All-American.

Football is Tom Thayer's life. Then again, so is surfing. He's an avid devotee of the sport, spending plenty of his off-season time on the Hawaiian island of Maui. Thayer joked that he's the best surfer from the 1985 Bears.

I've known Tom since he joined the Bears, and the guy you hear on the broadcasts is the same guy off it. He is the genuine article, a nice guy who happened to play in and now analyzes a very rough sport. Ask Tom to do a quick interview, and he never says no. Never! And when he starts talking, it's as if you're reading the encyclopedia of football. There isn't a question he can't answer. That and his pleasing voice make you think you're talking to your next-door neighbor. They should be as enjoyable as Tom is.

Tom had a very fruitful career with the Bears, playing in 133 games (including the playoffs and Super Bowl). But how he got to the Bears is quite a story.

"I had a weird journey getting to the Bears, because when I was in college and I was working out and went to all the combines and played a variety of positions at Notre Dame, I didn't know what I was going to be drafted for. It was a couple of days before the draft, and back in that era was super uneventful."

Thayer isn't kidding. It was just a day in the week, and they started the draft and kind of informed the player and who picked them, and they had no say in it. Today the draft is a three-day production in an NFL city with fan participation. It's quite a show.

"A week before the draft, I was walking out of the Notre Dame weight room, and I lived in the weight room. I'm thinking, *I'm gonna be one of those guys, I'm gonna get drafted high.* And Jim Parmer, who was one of the scouts for the Bears, I crossed paths with him in the hall at Notre Dame, and he said, 'Hey, I want to tell you something, I got good news. We had a mock draft the other day, and we drafted you in the fourth round!'"

This was not exactly the news Thayer was expecting.

"I said, 'Fourth round? That's crap! I'm not in the fourth. I'm going before that.'"

But just as suddenly as Thayer got the unsettling news came a more welcome option.

"Ironically enough, on the weekend, I get a call from George Allen and his son, Bruce Allen, who are running the Chicago Blitz [in the USFL]. They ended up calling my agent and asking if I was interested in a contract with the USFL. And I was so disappointed when I was told I [would be] drafted in the fourth round, I said, let's explore every option we can have because I believe I'm better than a fourth-rounder."

This saga has some twists and turns.

"George Allen devised this plan, saying, 'Don't tell anyone we're talking to you. Come out and meet me at the facility. Let's sign you to a contract, but don't tell anybody because it will give a chance for the USFL to make a big splash, to get a little bit of promotion on the cheap.'" The fledgling league was founded in 1983, so all the publicity it could get would help bolster its chances of actually competing with the NFL.

"I said fine. I was a young, naïve kid. They were going to offer me a guaranteed contract, which was basically unheard of at that time. So they offered me an opportunity to come to the USFL, sign a contract, leave school immediately, and go right to practice."

Now, Thayer's whirlwind football life was taking shape, albeit with an interesting caveat.

"That was on a Saturday. So Tuesday was the NFL Draft. As I had a news conference scheduled Tuesday with the Blitz, we had made the announcement I had signed a contract with the USFL to begin play immediately. After I made that announcement, my dad and I drove home from the Blitz facility, we pulled into the driveway, my sister came running out of the house, and said, 'Tom, [Bears GM] Jim Finks was on the phone. The Bears just drafted you.'

"I said, 'Oh, my God.' And my dad looked, and we were all kind of confused. It was in the fourth round. I was still disappointed because there were a couple of guys that got drafted ahead of me that I knew I was bigger, better, stronger, and more dedicated than, but it still fell on deaf ears, and there I was a fourth-round draft choice."

Thayer was in somewhat of a quandary, but money talks, and it talked loudly to the future Bear.

"At that point, I had signed a three-year, guaranteed, no-cut contract. However, when the Bears drafted me, they had my rights for four years. So here I am knowing that is my next best option after the USFL. If it folds or whatever happens after those three years, I will be able to negotiate with the Bears and sign there."

Thayer figured it didn't offer him any incentive. He had all the incentive he needed because he just wanted to play professional football. It was everything he had dedicated himself to.

"The next day, I loaded up my car and I drove up to the Chicago Blitz facility and started practice on that Wednesday. I became the starting right guard. And when I began playing there, I remember the first game I played was against the Washington Federals."

Imagine if the current Washington franchise had strongly considered Federals over Commanders? But I digress.

"I was 20 years old, and the guy I was playing against was a guy named Coy Bacon, and I think he was 40 at the time! I came in as a really competent kid, and I felt that my strength would get me through until I was up to the speed of the game. When I finished the season, I immediately re-enrolled in school, because I promised Father Hesburgh I would come back even though I withdrew from my senior year. I told him I would come back my first off-season and graduate."

And that's exactly what Thayer did. And immediately after graduating, he returned to the USFL.

"I played that season and knew in the off-season I was in for the long haul because the next season was the last year of my contract. It was fun, because in the second year we went to the championship game."

I believe earlier I mentioned twists and turns. Well, here's another example.

"The owner of the Chicago franchise was from Arizona, and the owner of the Arizona franchise was from Chicago, [and] they completely flipped. So we as the Chicago franchise became the Arizona Wranglers, and the Arizona team became the Chicago Blitz."

I don't know about you, but a couple of ibuprofen are in order.

"I wanted to stay with George Allen because George Allen was a huge, huge influence on my football preparation life. He was a defensive coach, but he taught me preparation week to week like no one I've ever played with before. So I went out to Arizona, where we lost to the Philadelphia Stars in the championship game. My third year we became the Arizona Outlaws, because we absorbed the Oklahoma Outlaws."

Forget the ibuprofen. Pass me something to drink with ice in it, and make it a double!

"It's kind of funny, because my first two years my quarterback was Greg Landry, who was a 40-year-old quarterback, and after the second year went on to sign with the Bears because they got to a desperate situation."

This was in 1984, when both Jim McMahon and his backup, Steve Fuller, got hurt.

"And from the Oklahoma Outlaws, our quarterback became Doug Williams!"

Williams would guide the Washington Redskins to victory in Super Bowl XXII. He was the first black QB to start and win a Super Bowl and was named the MVP.

"Williams was a tremendous, tremendous man. To this day, we are great friends. The lesson I learned from George Allen were non-repayable. But the lessons I learned from Greg Landry and Doug Williams were equally important."

So, finally, we get to the punch line or something akin to that.

"The final night we played in July, and we played in Tempe, where it was 113 degrees at kickoff. It was hot, and I remember in the fourth quarter they flashed a sign on the scoreboard the temperature has cooled down to 107 degrees! During the tail end of the season, I had signed my contract with the Bears, so I knew as soon as I was done with the game, my car was packed. I went from the locker room to my car and drove nonstop to Madison, Wisconsin. I went there and bought a Honda scooter, and I drove it to Platteville, Wisconsin, where the Bears held training camp. And the next Monday I began full pad practice with the Bears!"

This was the beginning of Thayer's NFL career, which crested early with a Super Bowl title in his first year.

Quite a saga, to say the least, but as many of us have learned, Tom Thayer is quite a guy.

# Hub Arkush

IT WAS a mid-August day in 2022. Hub Arkush was leaving Halas Hall after the Chicago Bears conducted one of their training camp practices. The longtime football writer and commentator had finished his work when suddenly, he collapsed. Arkush was suffering a heart attack, and if not for a security guard who was alerted that someone had gone down in front of the building, Arkush might have died. CPR and a defibrillator were used, and for a good 20 minutes. Arkush was rushed to a hospital, where he underwent a seven-hour surgery, spent some five weeks there, and then three more in a rehabilitation center. For a while, it was touch and go for the highly respected Arkush, who spent another four months trying to regain not only strength but his memory, as well. But thankfully for his readers, listeners, viewers, friends, and members of the media, Arkush returned to his myriad jobs. It was both a great relief and a joy.

Arkush has been writing about and commentating on pro football for over 40 years and is a premier authority on the sport. A man with plenty of opinions, he's not afraid to share them—witness his scathing rebuke of the Green Bay Packers quarterback Aaron Rodgers, who would go on to win the league's MVP award. Arkush admitted he didn't vote for him, saying he didn't think Rodgers could be the biggest jerk in the league, punish his team and fan base for the way he acts, and be the MVP. Arkush was administered his own rebuke in the media. He said he made a horrible mistake presenting things the way he did.

Arkush has had to deal with other mistakes and adversity during the course of his career, but he's managed to guide his way through them.

I've actually known Hub longer than anyone else in the media business, although neither of us had started on our professional paths then. It was sometime in 1973, when we both were attending Southern Illinois University. We were living in a complex called the Quads, and someone wanted to introduce us. Remember, this is the early 1970s. So there Hub was, sitting on a couch with hair down to his shoulders and a beard that would make Santa Claus jealous. I wouldn't run into Hub again until we were covering the Bears in the late 1970s/early '80s. And, yes, his hair was much shorter by then.

Hub is a straightforward guy with a nervous laugh, who happens to know just about everything there is to know about pro football. Over the years, watching, listening, and reading him is like eating your favorite meal. Very comforting.

While Hub loved sports and particularly football, he wanted to be an animal handler. He had become a certified lab tech at the University of Michigan's Unit for Laboratory Animal Medicine. He had no intentions of being in the football business. But story be told, life and death have a way of changing your outlook.

"It was just about that time my dad was beginning *Pro Football Weekly*," he told me. "The business was on death's door. We were struggling to even employ people. His circulation manager left unexpectedly."

This is when Arthur Arkush planted a seed in his son Herb's ear. Yes, Hub does have a real first name.

"'I know this is not what you're planning on doing,'" Hub remembered his father saying, "'but have you ever thought about it? Now would be a good time to give me a hand.'"

Arkush reluctantly turned down a job at the San Diego Zoo to work with his dad, who died unexpectedly just a few years later. So he ended up a journalist and broadcaster instead of an animal handler.

"Just a year before my father passed, he brought in some investment capital, enough to pay down all of our debt. But he also brought in his two closest confidants and friends in the NFL as consultants, Al Davis and Jim Finks."

Davis was the longtime and somewhat reviled owner of the Oakland Raiders, and Finks was the general manager who would be credited with building the 1985 Bears.

"They reached out to me and said, 'Whatever you need.' They became my counselors, my guidance. They taught me a ton about football, but also, as one of the most successful general managers and owners in NFL history, they taught me about running businesses. And there's no way I would have survived in the business at all without them!"

And through the years, the *Pro Football Weekly* business thrived. But it also had to navigate through a series of financial potholes.

"There were some hard times. We actually had to go through a bankruptcy six years after my dad passed away. That was as a result of the 56-day work stoppage in 1982. We managed to get through that and finally had some success through the '80s and '90s. So *Pro Football Weekly*, which was somewhat regarded as the bible of professional football, would not have attained that status had it not been for their contributions."

But the bumps continued, and in 1996 Arkush sold the business to a company that would become Primedia, the largest publisher of magazines in the world. The first three years, Arkush claims he was paid 10 times as much money as he was paying himself. Unfortunately, Primedia went bankrupt some seven or eight years later. But in 2003, Arkush bought the company back from Primedia.

"We had some new struggles because of the off-shore betting industry, so I sold it again in 2008 to GateHouse, who is actually the largest newspaper company in the country today."

GateHouse invested significant dollars, seeing the that future of the Internet was video and streaming.

"We built out video studios. We launched quite a bit of our own programming. Unfortunately, it got way ahead of the revenue stream, and GateHouse got into some issues as the magazine business was practically disappearing, and it decided to liquidate *Pro Football Weekly*."

You must be wondering at this stage why Arkush decided to stick with the business he'd invested so much time, energy, and aggravation in.

"At this stage I didn't have the stomach to start again from scratch, so I purchased the trademarks, copyrights, and IPs, and then simply went to work as an employee for Shaw Media, which is a large Illinois media group."

Through all of this, the *Pro Football Weekly* TV show has gone on uninterrupted.

Considering what Arkush had gone through over the course of some 40-plus years, I suggested he should write a book.

"My wife keeps telling me that. We'll see. One of these days. But the issue is to keep this thing going, I've always had four or five jobs at one time."

Arkush is now the senior columnist and analyst on the NFL for Shaw Media, the *Daily Herald*, and Paddock Publications. He's also an analyst on 670 The Score and working for Westwood One. What one hopes first is Arkush remains healthy.

And another hope: that he eventually writes that book, which I'm sure many will read.

# Dan Pompei

CONSIDER THIS for a moment: Dan Pompei, longtime football writer in Chicago, is on a committee to present evidence for a player who should be elected to the Pro Football Hall of Fame. Then, in 2013, Pompei himself was elected to the same Hall for his long and distinguished career as a writer and reporter. He was bestowed the Bill Nunn Memorial Award. Quite an achievement. Then again, Pompei is quite a gentleman. If members of the media could pick one writer in the city of Chicago to place on its highest pedestal, Pompei would be on or near the top. He's written countless stories about some of the premier and even some of the more nondescript players in the NFL. His career began with the *Chicago Sun-Times*. He would write for the *Sporting News*, eventually move to the *Tribune*, and then, several years ago, join The Athletic as their feature NFL writer. He's also written a book, *Fearless: How an Underdog Becomes a Champion*. The book chronicles the Philadelphia Eagles' run to a Super Bowl title in 2018.

Dan and I met during his early years covering the Bears, and it was easy to determine what a first-class pro he was even back then. Studious, intelligent, and graced with an immense amount of integrity, Dan quickly established himself as one of the top writers covering the Bears. His easygoing demeanor combined with his eloquent style of reporting made him someone you wanted to know whose brain you wanted to pick. Pompei gladly helped this reporter, whose weakness was football. I know, you're thinking, *Football is a weakness?* Well, compared to baseball, basketball, hockey, and tennis, it is.

What makes Dan so unique is that he's on this very important committee to argue on behalf of players to be elected to the Hall of Fame, and that is no easy task. But, of the five Chicago Bears he's campaigned for, four have gotten into the Hall, and the fifth, Devin Hester, is all but a shoe-in to eventually make it.

Dan relayed three stories: one about his very first assignment covering the Bears. The second about Walter Payton during his last season in 1987, and the third an absolutely hilarious tale about a Bears preseason game in 1988 that occurred in another country. But first, learn about how Pompei was pressed into service covering the Bears during his early years with the *Sun-Times*, and it happened to be 1985.

"As you might recall, the Bears got a little hot that year, and the two primary beat people at the *Chicago Sun-Times*, Kevin Lamb and Brian Hewitt, needed a little help on the beat, so I was recruited to help out. I was sent to New Orleans for Super Bowl XX [he's now been to 34 of the big games], but that one remains my most memorable for a number of reasons."

Unless you live deep under a rock, the Bears overwhelmed the New England Patriots 46–10, setting off pandemonium in Chicago.

"My assignment for that Super Bowl, and I was about one of 20 people that the *Sun-Times* sent down there, which at the time, seemed like a billion. I was assigned to cover the news, which was kind of like, okay, kid, go play in the street."

To say there were many story lines would be like saying a lot of potholes open up during a Chicago winter.

"Well, as it turned out, there was news, big news every day. Jim McMahon had an issue with a bruised rear end. He flew in his private acupuncturist, Hiroshi Shiriashi, and it was a drama all week [Shiriashi was flown in from Japan. He had previously treated Bears wide receiver Willie Gault]. Matter of fact, I was able to sneak into the room along with Johnny Morris from Channel 2 and his producer, Bob Vasilopoulos, as McMahon was getting acupuncture. We were in the room while he was getting needles stuck in his rear end."

This rather odd story had me chuckling throughout.

"Obviously, a different world back then, but the upshot was I had stories on the front page of the *Sun-Times* every day during that week. I was 24 years old, and it was my first real big splash, big bite of the apple, and my dear late mother, Nancy, took one of the front pages and wrote with a marker on it: 'You made it, Dan.' And she pointed to the byline on the front page, and I still have that page all these years later."

What a delightful and touching story.

Here's another touching, albeit not funny, story. It's about the final chapter of Walter Payton's great playing career.

"Walter, as you know, was a very elusive kind of guy. He was never one to sit still. He was always on the run and didn't like to share too much of himself. The season before Payton's last, they drafted Neal Anderson. And then, in 1987, they were kind of reducing Walter's role a little bit because they wanted to work Neal in, and Neal was a great talent. So Walter was kind of struggling with the whole idea of it, but he never said a word about it. He just kept putting his head down. He was doing what he had done for his entire incredible career."

Payton rushed for 1,333 yards on 321 carries in 1986. But in 1987, he rushed for only 533 yards and on 146 carries. Anderson carried the ball 129 times for 586 yards. His yards-per-carry was significantly higher than Payton's.

"One day, Payton is sitting in the locker room after practice. I walked in there with another reporter, and it was just the [three] of us. There was hardly anyone in the locker room. It was a strange day. Walter was sitting in his stall, and that's like, that's like finding a $100 bill on the sidewalk. We walked up to him, and he didn't walk away, which he usually would."

I know from experience that this is rare, and especially after a game when players usually disappear. Nowadays, the media is given access to only a handful of players.

"We sat down with him and asked him, 'What's going on?' It was clear he was emotional about what was happening.... He had his head literally in his hands and he was near tears talking about the frustration he was feeling and his career ending in a way he did not want it to end."

Payton was a very proud person. He had already become the league's all-time leading rusher and remains second only to Emmitt Smith to this day.

"He gave us a great story that day, and I remember the newspaper headline.... This was a front-page story in the *Sun-Times*. Those days, we were known for some of the sensational headlines, because Rupert Murdoch owned us, and the headline the next day on page 1 was, "Payton's Torment.""

Payton never said anything about it.

One year later, the Bears held that preseason game in Sweden, albeit with a different kind of torment.

"The Bears are playing the Vikings. They had one practice at one field. Then they told us they would have to move the practice the next day to another field. I guess the reason they had to move is the Vikings were on the field the Bears were being moved to, and they wanted out of there. They wanted to go the Bears' practice field to change things up. So the Bears moved."

There was a good reason why the Vikings wanted to move.

"The Vikings' practice field was next to a swimming pool."

Nothing wrong with that, right?

"In Sweden, it's a little different there, because women there are not necessarily required to wear tops at the pool."

Both Dan and I laughed, and then I interjected, "What an alluring practice session."

"Swedish women are known for their beauty, as well. So we walked onto the field, and I didn't see much practice that day, but one of the things I did see was a ball thrown and hitting a receiver in the side of the head because he was looking somewhere other than...so..."

Why do I get the feeling the next thing uttered by the players was, "Next man in the pool!"

Pompei continues to produce intriguing and worthwhile articles for The Athletic.

# BASKETBALL

# Bill Wennington

CAN YOU believe Bill Wennington once played hockey? Then again, if you're born in Montreal, one would assume you're born to play hockey. And Wennington did until he was 12. But he outgrew his skates and turned to basketball. Wennington was 6'2" and towered over the others he played with and against. Plus, in Canada the baskets were only eight feet high for 12-year-olds. But when Wennington came to the States, those baskets were 10 feet, and he struggled to score. He loved it just the same, enough to be recruited by St. John's and their legendary coach, Lou Carnesecca. He helped lead St. John's to a Final Four.

Wennington was selected in the first round of the 1985 NBA Draft by the Dallas Mavericks. Five years later, he was traded to the Sacramento Kings. Prior to joining the Chicago Bulls, Wennington played for a team in Italy and remembers it as a great experience. Then in 1993, he signed with the Bulls—only he didn't get a chance to play with Michael Jordan for nearly two years, as the iconic star decided to try his hand at baseball. Wennington would eventually win three titles with the Bulls and retired after the 1999–2000 season. For the past 19 seasons, Wennington has been a radio analyst for the Bulls, the last 15 alongside Chuck Swirsky.

Wennington played for the Canadian Olympic team and was inducted into the Canadian Basketball Hall of Fame.

Back in the 1990s, the Bulls locker room was full of players you could talk to, not the least of which was Jordan. It also included former Bulls executive John Paxson and current Golden State Warriors coach Steve Kerr. Bill was among those who were not only approachable but also gregarious. He was gracious and humorous, while also delivering the right sound bites for those of us in the electronic media. And when he became the Bulls analyst in 2003, nothing changed. Bill has remained this affable giant of a man. I can truly say *giant*, since he's 7' tall, and I'm just 5'7". Bill is also a fabulous storyteller, recounting episodes in his life with great clarity and of course, a generous amount of humor. Among the stories Bill remembered was Jordan's penchant for not only winning on the basketball court but in the gambling arena.

"That's another good story," he said. "The guys had their game of Tonk going on in the back of the plane."

Tonk is a card game featuring knock rummy and Conquain, which is a two-handed version of the game.

"One day, the usual crew—Scottie Pippen, Ron Harper, and Michael—were there. One time, there was someone who was gone and couldn't play."

Jordan knew Wennington could play Tonk, so obviously he was looking for another mark.

"Michael came up and said, 'We need one, so come back and play.' And he thinks I thought I would be a fish. When the game ended, I won 150 bucks. Everyone else broke even except Michael."

Remember, Michael hates to lose.

"Now, I'm talking 150 bucks, not thousands. We're talking $150, which is really nothing, especially for Michael at that time. He was not happy. He said, 'Get the bleep out of here, you're not playing with us anymore.' He wouldn't let me play."

Did I mention Jordan hated to lose?

"I came back a couple of times, and he said, 'You can't play, you're out, get out!'"

*Yikes.*

"So, again, someone else was gone, so he sent Scottie to me, and he said, 'You gotta come back and play.' So I came back to play, and at the end of that game, I lost $200, $250, and Michael had won. He goes, 'Now you'll never play again. Get the hell out of here!' It was one of two things: obviously, he understood I wasn't going to wager thousands of dollars, so I wasn't in that game. And he didn't like to lose, and at least that way he could walk away, winning."

That didn't deter Wennington from showering Jordan with praise.

"He was one of the most competitive guys I know, and I liked that about him because it shows how much he cares about winning, and it's his drive that made him, in my opinion, the best that ever played. People talk about how good he is, and I think they're underestimating him, I really do."

Underestimating him?

"What he did and—you want to talk about how hard he was on players?—well, he was hard on them because he was selfish and he wanted to be the best on the best team, but he wanted to win. And he wanted us to win as much as he wanted to win, so he was going to push us anyway he could.

"Jordan was more like a coach. When he saw players might be slacking or taking short cuts in practice, he'd let them know. And it's well-documented, Jordan would make it miserable on his teammates. His drive to win was insatiable.

"It would start off by just embarrassing us a little bit in practice, dunking on us, or if it continued verbally, it would go on even more."

This led to several skirmishes between Jordan and his teammates. Wennington said for him, it was great.

"I liked to think I understood it. Not to think I was smarter than everyone else, but I understood what was going on. He was like that parent or big brother who was pushing me because he saw something and wanted me to be better, like a coach would."

I mentioned that Wennington has quite a sense of humor. One of his classic lines came after Jordan dropped 55 points on the New York Knicks at Madison Square Garden. He also set up Wennington for a last-second, game-winning dunk. They were the only points Wennington scored, prompting him to say that he and Jordan combined for 57 points.

"I always knew I was a little bit funny. I know when I go back and visit my dad, I think I see where I got it. He was funny with a dry sense of humor. I don't know if I took it a step further, but I knew I could speak well."

I was lucky to get a floor seat on media row for most of the Jordan era, which of course, included Wennington, who was a vital part of a team boasting three Hall of Fame players—Jordan, Pippen, and Dennis Rodman—and a magnificent cast of supporting players. It was truly a pleasure, especially when interviewing Wennington. And thanks to his current role as the radio analyst, he remains very much part of that golden era of Bulls basketball.

# Chuck Swirsky

CHUCK SWIRSKY has always been a bit quirky—just check out his postgame dance when the Chicago Bulls win. Let's call it "freestyle," which has become rather popular on social media. Then again, Swirsky has been the popular radio voice of the Chicago Bulls since 2008. He arrived the same season Derrick Rose did. Timing is everything. Prior to that he was the voice of the Toronto Raptors. His résumé speaks of many travels and achievements. His career began in Columbus, Ohio, where he did a nighttime sports talk show. Suddenly, a headhunter called, telling him of a 50,000-watt station in the Midwest. Swirsky hung up, thinking it was a prank, but the headhunter called back minutes later and told him not to do that again! He was offering Swirsky a chance at a lifetime. It happened to be WCFL, now WMVP–ESPN 1000. Just 24, Swirsky was now in a major market, where he didn't know the teams, and the fans certainly didn't know him. He was ridiculed by members of the media, who didn't take him seriously, and he barely got a fan phone call those first few months. Swirsky admitted he was scared out of his mind. But not only did he survive, he flourished. That led him to WLUP radio; then being public address announcer for the Bulls; WGN radio, where he did pre- and postgame for Bears broadcasts; and eventually the play-by-play voice for DePaul University basketball. Swirsky was also mocked by Bruce Wolf, a creative sportscaster who would parody his voice, something Swirsky was not too fond of. But it managed to enhance his persona.

Then it was on to Detroit where he called University of Michigan basketball. That stop led him to Toronto and his first NBA gig. Chuck was elected to the Chicagoland Sports Hall of Fame in 2016, and in 2022 wrote a book titled *Always a Pleasure*, with a portion of the proceeds going to charity.

Swirsky is well liked and admired by his fans and peers for his positive attitude. He's always tweeting messages like, "Happy Friday! Keep grinding. Keep believing in yourself and don't allow discouragement to deter you from your ultimate goal." He also encourages aspiring broadcasters to send him audiotapes so he can guide them in the right direction.

I first came into contact with Chuck when he arrived in 1979. I was 25 and had already begun my freelance career. While covering the Hambletonian, the premier triple crown race for standardbreds then raced in downstate Du Quoin, I convinced Chuck to let me do a report for him. From there, we were part of the late Les Grobstein's radio all-star baseball team. It was a wonderful way for many of us just getting started in the business to get to know one another. When Chuck returned to Chicago to become the voice of the Bulls, I would see him often while covering games, and he exuded the positive attitude that has become his trademark.

Unlike most of us, Chuck didn't grow up in a sports-oriented atmosphere. He was born in Norfolk, Virginia, but grew up in Bellevue, Washington.

"My father was a naval officer and had zero interest in sports, zero!" Chuck said. "He was a man of great character and integrity. He was on the base quite a bit and loved to work on cars. But the only time we played ball in the backyard with a baseball and a glove— very seldom. My mom was a school teacher, zero interest in sports.

"It was May, one month away from leaving elementary school and going into junior high school. I come home on a Wednesday, and my father was home and he says, 'Charley'—people referred to me as Charley, I was never called Chuck until college—'why don't we go to a ballgame tonight?'"

Swirsky was obviously stunned.

"I said, 'What, dad?' And he said, 'We're going to a ballgame.' Now, at that time, Seattle did not have a major league team. This was 1966, and the Seattle Angels, a Triple A club, played at Sicks Stadium. So my dad takes me to a ballgame against Salt Lake City.

We leave about the sixth inning or seventh inning because I had school the next day."

Then came news any child would dread. Swirsky was in the sixth grade.

"Twenty-four hours later, I was pulled out of class at lunch-time. My school teacher, Mr. Filler, calls me out in the hallway and says, 'Charley, I regret to inform you, your father passed away this morning.'"

Swirsky fainted and later said he was back in his house and didn't know how he got from point A to point B.

"My brain was completely dark, and there is my mom weeping. My two sisters are around. My neighbors are there, and it was like, wow! I think about that story, because my father, who was not a sports fan, completely out of the blue took me to a baseball game just before his death. And I think about what that means, and I'm still at times trying to figure it out nearly 60 years later. All I can tell you is a story that is in my heart forever."

"It's a sad story," I said, "but an inspiring one, as well."

"Yeah, it is. My parents and the way I try to raise my children, who are all adults now, is that my father always put his children ahead of himself. And the one thing I try to plant the seed [of] with a lot of people in our industry is, from generation to generation, the greatest impact you can have on a person is to give of yourself.

"My first mentor in this business was Vince Bagli, who died in 2020 at the age of 93. I met him after my father died. My uncle lived in Baltimore, where he knew the Bagli family. Vince was the dean of sports there."

This is where Swirsky's life changed again, just months after his father died.

"I stayed with Vince, his wife, and their six kids every summer. I would go to the station and sit next to him and do everything he asked me to do, whether it was to find slides for his TV appearance to ripping copy from the wire machines. Mentorship is extremely important."

This is why Swirsky reaches out to young aspiring announcers and offers himself to them. He endears himself to people no matter who or where they are.

Chuck Swirsky. Big talent. Big heart!

# Lisa Byington

LISA BYINGTON is a trailblazer, even though she declines to except the moniker. She's the first female to be a lead announcer for a professional men's franchise, the Milwaukee Bucks. And she was the first female to call an NCAA men's basketball tournament game. Ask how best to describe these achievements, and Byington replied, "I'm a broadcaster." And she's a pretty good one at that. Byington also calls the Chicago Sky of the WNBA, along with other assignments. She's forever grateful to the Chicago Bulls, who auditioned a number of candidates to replace the retiring Neil Funk. She got a chance to do several games alongside Bulls analyst Stacey King. The job eventually went to Adam Amin.

A native of Portage, Michigan, Byington began her career in the tiny town of Alpena, Michigan, the second smallest TV market in the country! She earned $14,000 a year and wouldn't look at her paycheck because it depressed her. But this is where she learned her craft. She climbed the ladder, where she also learned never to say no to an opportunity—take the grunt job to get the glory job, and that's where Byington is today.

I had never met Lisa, but it was Dave Revsine, the outstanding host of the Big Ten Network, who suggested I interview her since she went to Northwestern. Little did I realize that she was a student-athlete the same time Pat Fitzgerald was one of the nation's top linebackers. This was one those requests that turned out be like finding sunken treasure at the bottom of Lake Michigan. Lisa was an avid fan of my podcast, so there was an instant camaraderie. She spoke highly of my work, while I already felt the same about hers.

And she was a great interview. Lisa is humble, downplaying the firsts she's achieved in the industry. She was reflective about her career but also thankful for where it's taken her. And she recalled how she finally made one of her breakthroughs while also dealing with what is still a male-dominated industry.

"I had a dream of working the NCAA Tournament," she said, "but at the time it was only as a sideline reporter. I had not been a play-by-play announcer at that point. As a kid, the NCAA Tournament was my Super Bowl because that's what I grew up watching. So, as a broadcaster, I said, 'You know what? I want to work the tournament.' So, in 2007, I was working in local news. I was in Lansing, Michigan, at the time. I went down to Atlanta. I knew enough people to introduce me to the right person to get myself in front of that CBS executive."

Byington wasn't going down to see the games. Her sole purpose was to meet someone who would fulfill her dreams. Byington hopped into her car and made the 11-hour drive to Atlanta.

"I booked a hotel outside Atlanta because staying close to the arena was much too much for me to afford. Finally, I got in front of Michael Rosen, who was one of the ones in charge of CBS at the time. I introduced myself...and I know he's sitting there thinking, *Who is this random local sports person?* Let's be honest, they get that all the time."

Byington made enough of an impression that, many months later, she got a phone call from New York. And she thought this was her NCAA Tournament call. Not exactly.

"It was Ross Molloy, who is still there, and he said, 'Lisa, I'd like to offer you a sideline job on our Division II football package that we air on CBS Sports Network on Thursday night.'"

Byington was wondering, jokingly, whether there was anything coming after this seven-game package.

"At the time, I didn't say no to anything, because at the time anything was an opportunity. So, of course, I said yes. And, of course, it was one of the most challenging jobs because it was hard to get information on Division II schools. You know what it did? It opened up the door. CBS kept me on their radar, and every year, every year, I wrote an email to CBS and Turner Sports: 'I'd love to be a sideline reporter for the NCAA Tournament.'"

Byington's persistence finally paid off.

"Ten years later, I get an email, and I almost deleted it because I thought it was spam for my cable package. So I clicked on it, and it was the email I always wanted. It was the email I was searching for in 2007. We would love you to be one of our sideline reporters this year for the NCAA Tournament. Would you be interested?"

This is where the tiresome though apt cliché comes into play: "*Are you kidding me?*"

"I love that story for this: a lot of great things have happened to me, especially in the most recent past, and I think that's what people see sometimes who don't know my story. Lisa Byington has done this and this. People don't realize what it takes to get to that job. You pursue it, you work hard, and handle people the right way, I'd like to say those dreams happen. It took 10 years in the making but I never gave up on it."

During her quest to reach her dreams, Byington also had to deal with the nightmare of chauvinism in the broadcast business.

"Every day," she said. "And sometimes people show it without meaning to show it. Here's an example of that: we went down, the Bucks were playing the Heat in Miami. There was an audio technician who came up to me and introduced himself, and he said, 'I got all your sideline reporter stuff set up on this side of the baseline.'"

Oops.

"I had to put my hand up to stop him. I know I'm blonde, and you see a lot of blonde females on the sideline, but I had to stop him in mid-sentence. You know, I'm sorry, I have to interrupt, but I'm not the sideline reporter, I'm the play-by-play. He stopped in his tracks, and a look of horror came across his face. And I realized at the time, based on his reaction, he wasn't trying to be a jerk, but what was his normal? His normal was, anytime you see a female on a TV crew, that female was always a sideline reporter."

Byington fit a stereotype. So this was what his normal was.

"There are times where people are sometimes chauvinistic when they don't mean to be or don't try to be. There are other examples your listeners need to hear about. People will come up, and they'll compliment me, and they really enjoyed my broadcasts this year. 'You really sound like you know what you're talking about.'"

Byington will smile and say thank you, but to her that's not always a 100 percent compliment, and you can understand why.

"If I'm a male announcer, is that the first thing you're going to try to figure out about this new announcer? Do they know what they're talking about? Usually, with male announcers, people skip over that part. But I've noticed with female announcers, it always starts there."

Point taken. I, for one, care more about substance than style. I've heard the likes of others, including Beth Mowins and analysts such as Sarah Kustok and Doris Burke, and they have become part of the landscape. They're not women who simply know what they're talking about, they're broadcasters who know what they're talking about. The understanding of women play-by-play and game analysts is the thing of the present and growing. So are female referees in the NBA and NFL.

And that's a good thing.

# Adam Amin

IF YOU haven't heard of Adam Amin by now, you're not a sports fan. But if you're not a follower of sports, Amin is native Chicagoan whose meteoric rise in the broadcast business is no surprise. He is the current voice of the Chicago Bulls, where he teams up with the uproarious Stacey King to provide viewers a very entertaining broadcast. It's so entertaining, you can hear Amin's high-pitched laughter often after King delivers some of his witty commentary. Amin is also one of the premier play-by-play men for Fox on its coverage of the NFL and Major League Baseball, this after a successful stint at ESPN. But like many in the industry, Amin started his career in college, at Valparaiso University, where he also called minor league baseball. After stops in Wisconsin and Iowa, ESPN hired him in 2011, where one of his assignments was the famous Nathan's Hot Dog Eating Contest. We're happy to tell you the diminutive Amin declined to be one of the contestants. Amin also called the Women's NCAA Final Four before departing for Fox.

Amin's upbeat style has become a hit with fans in Chicago and around the nation. He's part of a breed of 30-something announcers who have blanketed the national scene, and they include another Chicagoan, Jason Benetti, the voice of the White Sox and Fox Sports. Benetti will sometimes fill in for Amin on Bulls games when he's on a network assignment.

Adam was the first guest on my podcast whom I had never met. Our paths hadn't crossed, but we knew of each other's work. So I invited him out to dinner, and we got to know one another. I quickly realized what a charming and motivated person Adam is. I also realized we had several things in common. We are both the youngest in our families and the only ones born in the United States. And we are both 5'7". Though I didn't ask, I suspect Adam can't dunk a basketball, either! At this point, Adam was also the youngest guest I had interviewed, and it was about time I talked to someone under 40!

Besides discussing common friends in the industry and living in the city, we got around to Adam's background and the immigration of his father from Pakistan, a story of perseverance and family loyalty.

"My father was a very sharp man," Adam said. "He was the vice president of a bank in Karachi, Pakistan. He was well off with a good job, played semipro cricket, a sport he loved."

But during that time, in that culture and religion, there was a desire for marriage.

"There was an arrangement that worked out well with his 16-year-old wife, my mom. She was from a very poor part of Pakistan, not very well off, larger family...and I've gotten to know this over the years since my dad died, my mom was very sharp, too, but didn't get a chance to explore that because she came from a poor family."

Luckily for Adam and his brothers, his mom and dad got a chance to get to know and become fond of one another, something you might think would be a lot more difficult in an arranged marriage. They were married in 1968 and had three boys before Adam—one in 1969, another in 1973, and a third in 1979. They were a very established family, but that's when things changed, and dramatically.

"For whatever reason, [my dad] and his brother, who also had a wife and a couple of kids, they decided to establish a life in America."

Life in South Asia and the Middle East was becoming volatile in the late 1970s, and the situation was punctuated when Iran held more than 50 Americans hostages for 444 days.

"Part of the move to the United States was the American dream, and over the years my dad became deeply American. He really appreciated the opportunity to come here, but it's kind of drastic to think he was 40 years old at this point. So here he is with an established life and family and leaving Pakistan to go thousands of miles to the United States and become a manual laborer. So he and his brother came to Chicago and worked at a factory that molded and shaped windows that went into high-rise buildings in downtown Chicago."

This is where Amin lives now and says he can't help but laugh when he looks at one of the buildings and wonders whether one of those was one his dad and uncle made windows for. While this was going on, mind you, his mom and three of his uncles were still in Pakistan!

"My dad goes from being this well-to-do man, white-collar job, to being a blue-collar guy every day and is still the most impressive employee! He and his brother would outwork a lot of the people who were there, and the boss was under the impression they couldn't speak English. My dad and his brother spoke pretty god English."

Adam's dad worked hard enough to earn a much-needed raise.

"I'm convinced that if I got anything from him, it was his work ethic. Here he is in America while Mom and the three kids are by themselves in Pakistan. Obviously, they're being taken care of, but they're by themselves, and she's raising three kids, one who is a very small child, and they have very little communications."

Collect calls were out of the question because he had to save every penny. The more he saved, the quicker he could get his family to join him in Chicago.

"For seven years, until 1985, they talked maybe once a year, and there would be a couple of letters back and forth every month. And my mom still has a box of those letters she would probably have a hard time looking at."

Adam was born in 1986 and named by his three brothers, the oldest of whom was only 17. What a way to join a family that just recently arrived in the U.S.

"My two younger brothers were very enthusiastic, so I don't blame my older brother, who was about to go to college...we were never destined to be attached by the hip, but all of them put a lot of investment into me. And when I was born my dad was 50."

Here's another way Adam and I are somewhat attached. My dad and mom arrived to this country in 1951 after fleeing war-torn Europe. They had no money, two young kids, and didn't speak a lick of English. I came into being some two and a half years later.

"My dad and two younger brothers were very protective of me. My three brothers have very strong, traditional Pakistani/Muslim names: Ismail, Abdullah, and Mustafa. They had gone to school here for about a year and got plenty of ridicule, as plenty of kids would in the '80s. They sensed they didn't want that for me. My mom wanted to name me after my father, whose name was Mohmmad, but my brothers all declared, 'We cannot do this to him.' They wanted to take take a little pressure off me, off any any reputation I might have to battle through by giving me an Americanized yet still Quranic name."

So Adam it was. There was enough appeal to his mother and logic to his brothers to name him that.

Adam's father died in 2018.

# Will Perdue

WILL PERDUE has four NBA championship rings. That's more than Toni Kukoč, Bill Wennington, John Paxson, and even Dwyane Wade! Perdue won three with the Bulls and another with the San Antonio Spurs. Not bad for a guy almost no one heard of when he was drafted by the Bulls with the 11th pick in the first round of the 1988 draft. Perdue suffered through a bumpy ride with the Bulls yet contributed to three of their six titles. Raised in Merritt Island, Florida, Perdue was a gawky kid who didn't invest in the game of basketball until he was 13 because his elementary school did not have a gym! His dad built a hoop on the back of the garage, and that's where Perdue learned to play. But thanks to a friend, he was able to hone his skill. Perdue didn't make his seventh-grade team despite standing 6'1". He did make his eighth-grade team but wasn't very good. But his game and height improved in high school.

Perdue was recruited by Vanderbilt, where he emerged as a star player and, in 1988, was named the SEC Player of the Year and conference male athlete of the year!

Perdue spent 13 seasons in the NBA and, in subsequent years, began his career in broadcasting, which included doing college games for Westwood One. Over the last several years, Perdue has been a Bulls studio analyst, along with Kendall Gill and Jason Goff.

I covered Will during his years with the Bulls and have watched his very cogent analysis. He is a very amiable, straightforward person who also harbors some bitterness going back to the days when he was drafted by then Bulls GM Jerry Krause. It was a curious pick, since few experts expected Perdue to be chosen that high. That was 35 years ago, but Perdue can't shake how he was treated.

"I don't want to use the word *hatred*, but when I came here for my press conference, I remember all the negative questions. If I didn't know any better, these guys think I'm a high school player or something. I got no skills. I just got drafted 11th in the NBA Draft. Do they not understand what I accomplished in college and how I busted my ass to get here?"

I was at that press conference, and the negative questions were indeed overwhelming. But though the criticism was really aimed at Krause, it was Perdue who felt as if he were a sitting duck.

"I always felt in this market as if I was always having to climb uphill. It was all part of the process, but I felt the story in the *Tribune* and *Sun-Times* set the tone for what the fans thought of me, as well."

It did and translated to some of the players, including Michael Jordan.

"And there's always the famous story, Michael refused to call me 'Will Perdue' because I wasn't good enough to be considered to be a player from the Big Ten, so he called me 'Will Vanderbilt.' That bothered me and, quite honestly, affected me as a player when I was here. I had to fight a lot of inner demons, and I always thought, *What if I went to San Antonio with Gregg Popovich beforehand?*"

Ironically, Perdue would eventually be traded to the Spurs for Dennis Rodman, and Popovich would be his coach. But Perdue was dealing with more than just being ostracized by media, fans, and teammates.

"There was also the turmoil surrounding Doug Collins [Bulls head coach from 1986 to 1989]. There were a lot of people who said, 'Guess what? Perdue got Collins fired.'"

Collins was fired in July 1989, though it had nothing to do with Perdue. Team owner Jerry Reinsdorf thought he saw the disintegration of the team under Collins so he hired assistant coach Phil Jackson to take over.

Perdue was incredulous about the rumors. "What did I do?" he responded emphatically. "I always felt like I was kind of the guy that, if something went wrong, it was my fault. Internally, I didn't handle it very well. I could see these stories about people always saying I wouldn't change a thing. Well, I would personally change a lot!"

The internal issues Perdue was dealing with also became external. Practices with Michael Jordan were intense. Sometimes, a bit too intense.

"What people don't know is that was commonplace. Not necessarily guys getting punched but the volatility, the competitiveness, the aggression...that's what made us so good. That was commonplace, where guys had to be held back, pushing matches, shoving matches because we would go through our skills work, but you always ended practice with a scrimmage. That atmosphere was set by Michael. And everyone tried to live up to those expectations, not only of him and the coaching staff but of yourself. It was a constant battle."

As it turned out during one rather competitive practice, Jordan warned Perdue that, if he banged him during another screen, he'd make him pay for it. Perdue did, knocking Jordan to the floor. Jordan got up and punched Perdue, who was ready to retaliate until cooler heads prevailed. Jordan did apologize, but Perdue admitted, "He got me pretty good."

Perdue also wasn't much of a fan of Phil Jackson's, so when he was traded to the Spurs for Dennis Rodman, he considered it a blessing.

"The biggest thing about Pop [Popovich] was two things: one, Pop dumbed things down, where he made it easier, not harder. But for me, the biggest thing about Pop was, you really felt like he cared about you as a person. You weren't just a basketball player to him; you weren't just a guy trying to help him win games. It started from day one. Pop was the general manager, and Bob Hill was the coach. As pissed off as I was when I got traded, which was after Michael came back and we lost to Orlando in the playoffs, you knew what was coming."

The Bulls needed better rebounding, and despite Rodman's past, especially against the Bulls, he replaced Perdue.

"I'm not a gambling man, but if I was, I would have bet any penny we had the Bulls winning a championship. And a week before the season, *boom*, I get traded."

In fact, it was the start of the Bulls' second threepeat.

"I get traded, and it's demoralizing. I'm not happy, but when I get to San Antonio, we go to training camp the next day. Pop sits me down and looks me square in the eye and says, 'Listen, we traded for you for a reason. The Bulls tried to give us other players.' Whether this was BS or not doesn't matter, though I didn't think it was BS because Pop was honest. He was brutally honest, only in a fatherly type of way. 'We traded for you because we think there are things you can do to help this team you were not allowed to do in Chicago."

Perdue's minutes increased, as did his rebounds during his four seasons with the Spurs, and they won the title in the 1998–99 season. Perdue then re-signed with the stripped-down Bulls, who, after winning their sixth title in eight years in the 1997–98 season, saw Michael Jordan retire again, only to eventually make a comeback with the Washington Wizards. Then Perdue began his second and current career as an analyst. He appears happy and content these days so long as you don't bring up those early days with the Bulls.

# Cassidy Hubbarth

DID YOU know Cassidy Hubbarth was a three-sport athlete at Evanston Township High School? Now she's interviewing top-notch athletes in the NBA. Hubbarth is a premier talent on ESPN, where she's a full-time reporter throughout the league's regular season and playoffs. She's interviewed all the biggest stars—LeBron James, Giannis Antetokounmpo, Steph Curry, you name it. And she does it with class and integrity. Whether it's a long-form interview or short-burst sideline report, Hubbarth has established herself among the elite in the business.

And to think, Hubbarth began her career as a traffic reporter and producer for a local TV station in Chicago. It didn't take her long to move to her passion, sports. She worked at Comcast Sports-Net Chicago (now NBC Sports Chicago), the Big Ten Network, and Fox Sports before joining ESPN in 2010.

Born and raised in Evanston, Illinois, Hubbarth was part of Evanston Township High School's state soccer championship team. And, like so many in the media business, she graduated from North-western's prestigious Medill School of Journalism.

Her busy schedule includes being a mother. She gave birth to a girl in 2018.

I had never met Cassidy. It was suggested I do my podcast with her by Lisa Byington, the voice of the Milwaukee Bucks and Chicago Sky, and a previous guest.

Good idea.

All it took was one email and a subsequent phone call. She was gung-ho. Her enthusiasm was contagious and especially when discussing how she gave a commencement speech for her high school and did so virtually during the COVID pandemic. What I came to learn about Cassidy is her enthusiasm and dedication to her craft.

So two interesting stories here. The first is that commencement speech, which was quite different from many others, and her first NBA sideline interview with a coach who loathes doing them.

"I kind of had an easy introduction to Gregg Popovich," she recalled, "because I was doing the game with P.J. Carlesimo, who was on his staff. We usually sit down with coaches before the game and get a low-down on their teams, and Carlesimo made an introduction, telling Popovich, 'You gotta take it easy on my girl.'

"Of course, this led Popovich into a whole rant about why he doesn't like these interviews, and if you've ever watched him doing them, you would clearly understand. There are probably very few sideline reporters at any network who likes doing these interviews, but it gives them access, and once in a while news emanates from them.

"Popovich uses these interviews to take it out on the lowest person on the totem pole, which is not right. He uses those moments to make a protest against the league for doing it. But he told me, 'There are only two questions that you should be asking in those interviews—what didn't you like? and what do you hope to improve on?—because I'm not going to give away my observations or strategies.'"

You're probably wondering if there's any other NBA coach who determines what a reporter should ask. What made this just a little different is, it was a special day on the NBA calendar.

"Maybe because it was Christmas, I can get him to smile. I had him in the first quarter, which is better than having him in the third quarter, because...the third is heading into a decisive fourth. But, as the time was winding down in the first quarter, the Spurs were losing and not playing very well. And so I'm like, 'Oh, man!' I go up to him, and I'm so nervous I think my mic was shaking, and I asked my first question, 'What do you hope to improve on first-quarter play?' I think I said it 50 miles an hour! I just spit it out, and he actually gave me an answer. It wasn't a long answer, but he said, 'Pick-and-roll defense.' I didn't need him to go on and on, just have your body language respectful. Then I said, 'For Christmas, I'm not going to ask you a second question as a gift.' He smiled and said thank you."

Hubbarth got Pop to smile, and it was a moment for her. She lucked out because she had the whole Christmas spirit thing on her side.

Hubbarth displayed another spirit in 2021. It was her school spirit. She had attended Evanston Township High School and was asked to deliver the commencement speech but because of COVID, it turned out to be a very unique speech.

"It was special. I felt for those kids, because it was a dream of mine to do the commencement speech. Graduation is usually during the playoffs, so it was hard for me to do the commencement speech and not to conflict with playoff games. So, when they asked me to do the speech, and it was still going to be over Zoom, I said I have to do it. I felt so bad these kids losing two years of their high school life and having their commencement on a computer screen."

But Hubbarth didn't want to do the usual speech. She wanted it to be different, one of the reasons why she's been a successful broadcaster.

"I hired one of the production assistants I worked with on *Hoop Streams*, and I was like, can you help me edit one of these videos and add some fun graphics so it stands out more than someone talking on Zoom in their commencement? I think it turned out okay. I had some students reach out. I wanted to make it feel somewhat special to them after what was probably a couple of very difficult years for them, not being able to experience their junior and senior years, which were two of the best years of my life."

I saw the video and told Cassidy that, put into sports terms, it was a game-winning three-pointer from halfcourt. It was very impressive. She thanked me profusely, but it was really not necessary. It was truly a joyful work of art.

Then Hubbarth remembered how the high school had bestowed an honor on her.

"They gave me an alumnus award a few years ago, and I was able to work off of that and was able to dig up some core memories at ETHS and work into the commencement speech. The reason my speech was so successful is that ETHS helped me chase my dreams and provided so many opportunities for me to explore this thing that I knew was inside me."

Hubbarth was a member of the radio-TV club in high school and got to do boys' basketball. She had the footage, and being able to show her growth, when she was interviewing LeBron James resonated with people.

Sometimes high school doesn't fill that bill for everyone, but sometimes it does. Witness Cassidy Hubbarth, who has blossomed into one of the business's best in-game interviewers. But you need more than that. You need personality, as well, and my interview with Hubbarth provided that and then some.

# Porter Moser

HE WILL forever be linked with Loyola, a magic carpet ride, and a wildly popular nun. Porter Moser, now head coach at Oklahoma, brought the Jesuit school on the banks of Lake Michigan to the forefront of college basketball when he guided his Ramblers to the 2018 Final Four. It was an extraordinary, gut-wrenching, high-drama journey that not only caught Chicago by surprise but college basketball fans all over the country. But it was Sister Jean who caught the attention of the entire world. The Ramblers would lose in the semifinals, but Moser would eventually get a more lucrative job in Norman, Oklahoma.

Born and raised in Naperville, Illinois, Moser's rise to prominence came with many potholes, but this charismatic and died-in-the-wool Chicago sports fan managed to achieve what many coaches only dream of. His story is of basketball—playing, coaching, and loving the sport that gained him deserving publicity. His trek as a coach took him to Little Rock, Arkansas; Illinois State; St. Louis; and then to Sheridan Road on the North Side of Chicago, where Loyola resides. Moser suffered through three straight losing seasons before the Ramblers got an invite to the College Basketball Invitational, which they won! Three years later, he made the valiant attempt to bring Loyola its second national championship. Its first came in 1963 under head coach George Ireland.

Moser spurned several offers to leave after the Final Four run, saying he had a hole in his belly and didn't want to win and run. He stayed at Loyola until 2021, when he decided to make his move and join Oklahoma.

There are few men I've been around and enjoyed more than Porter. Besides being charismatic, his vibrant and enthusiastic personality easily grabs you. It's hard not to admire these qualities.

*Porter Moser with the author*

He's a magnet as you clasp onto his every word. He can be jovial but also stern, witness when his team isn't playing up to its capabilities. But he's also a cheerleader, and not just for Loyola during his 10-year stint. He's such a devout Chicago sports fan. His devotion, particularly to the Cubs, oozes out of his veins. The run to the Final Four revealed Moser's stout yet engaging characteristics. I remember interviewing him in his office and then on the floor of the Gentile Arena, where Loyola plays its games. His desire to be involved is all but unmatchable. It's one of the main reasons talking to him is such a pleasure.

And so was the podcast we did. We went through the difficult loss to Michigan in the semifinals of the Final Four and, of course, Sister Jean. How could we not?

"We're talking about something I think about a lot," Moser said. "I can tell you every play down the stretch. It took me 'til the pandemic, when I watched the game over! That's the truth. It took me two years to rewatch the Michigan game because we believed, we believed we were going to win the national championship. When we were paired against Miami in the first round, we weren't saying we're going to the Final Four. Then there was Tennessee, and we weren't saying we're going to the Sweet 16. But when we got to the Final Four, I thought we were going to win the national championship."

Consider the road the Ramblers took during the tournament to get to the Final Four. They won the first game over Miami by two points on a buzzer-beater by Donte Ingram. They beat Tennessee in the next game on a shot by Clayton Custer with 3.6 seconds left to win 63–62. If that wasn't the stuff heart attacks are made of, Loyola advanced to the Elite Eight with a 69–68 win on a Marques Townes's three-point shot with 6.2 seconds left. So they won the first three games by a combined four points! But they managed to coast to the Final Four with a 16-point victory over Kansas State.

Then came the semifinal against No. 3 seed Michigan.

"We were up 10 in the second half," Moser recalled. "And we had seven bad possessions in a row! It was just a really, really bad run. Aundre Jackson was a huge factor all season. And if you add up the five games in the tournament, he was the leading scorer. Never led us in one game, but he was crucial in every game."

But Jackson injured his knee on the very first play as he drove down the lane.

"He kind of limps back and doesn't say anything to us. He tries to fight through it, but when you really watch the game, he was totally ineffective. When we got back a couple of days later, they did an MRI, and Aundre tore his meniscus. The doctor said, 'I don't know how he played.' It was unfortunate for him, but we were right there. I think about it a lot, and it drives me to be on that stage again."

The stage didn't belong solely to Moser and his team. As a matter of fact, there were times when it felt like the Ramblers were pushed off the stage by the venerable Sister Jean. She was 98 at the time, and who knew the stir she would cause and the immense publicity she would get around the world as Loyola kept moving on in the tournament.

"I knew of Sister Jean, but she wasn't 'Sister Jean' to the world until the tournament. All the media hype going into the tournament wasn't about her. Donte [Ingram] hits the shot against Miami, we all go crazy, we celebrate, we go up to our fans, and we're walking off the floor, and Tom Hitcho had wheeled Sister Jean down there, and we're walking off the floor and every single person is giving her a hug. And that's how it started. Forty-eight hours later, it was worldwide. It was insanity. And I remember it got so crazy, we're playing Tennessee, and we're doing our prayer. Sister was in her chair, and we all interlocked arms and we're about to do this, and Bill Behrns, our SID, says to me, 'Porter, the media wants to be in on this prayer.'"

Moser was incredulous. He said all week she did interviews, and something's got to be sacred. But sacred was tossed out the window. Ninety-eight-year-old Sister Jean was becoming an international star.

"I looked down the tunnel, and they it roped off, and it's like eight deep of cameras and people. And they're all down there like a bunch of people waiting for a little bone. Right when I told Bill something's got to be sacred, Sister says, 'Hey, let 'em down, come on in.' She's waving them down."

I blurt out, "She's a star!" But still Porter doesn't want anything to do with this.

"So I'm like, I'm gonna put my foot down. I'm trumping this. I said, 'All right, no cameras inside the circle.' Like, here I am trying to get a little authority in this situation when I lost all authority. And I'm telling you, I'm looking around, and every shoulder and between every person's leg was a camera! And all you heard was Sister Jean: "Goodness gracious God." And you're hearing the shuttering of cameras. I grew up Catholic, but this is putting this Catholic thing on a stage, like we're trying to exploit this thing."

The laughter is flowing as Moser tries to continue the story. It was quite a phenomenon. Sister Jean almost upstaged Moser's team!

"If she was on this podcast with me," he said, "you know what she would say? 'What do you mean *almost*?'"

And we laugh at it.

"When some reporter told her, 'You're nationally famous now,' she corrected him: 'No, I'm worldwide!'"

Loyola didn't make the tournament in 2023, after going 25–8 in Drew Valentine's first season as Moser's replacement. As for Sister Jean, she was still going strong at 103!

# Sarah Kustok

SARAH KUSTOK is a vibrant, personable, and exceptionally talented broadcaster who also is a trailblazer. She became the first female analyst for an NBA team when hired by the YES Network to work Brooklyn Nets games. Kustok works seamlessly alongside veteran play-by-play announcer Ian Eagle. Kustok arrived from Chicago, where she fashioned a career as a TV anchor and reporter for Comcast SportsNet in Chicago, where one of her biggest roles was covering the 2010 Stanley Cup–champion Blackhawks.

Kustok is a native of Orland Park, a southwest suburb of Chicago. She made her mark as a college basketball player in the early 2000s. She starred at DePaul under head coach Doug Bruno, who is still there and was also a guest on my podcast. Meanwhile Kustok's brother, Zak, also was a college athlete, having been a quarterback at Northwestern. Kustok helped the Blue Demons to four post-season appearances and was also a team captain. She was one of its top three-point shooters. In 2005 she was named an assistant coach under Bruno, but that didn't last very long. When a future in basketball was not in the cards, Kustok turned to the world of broadcasting. She met with some officials at ESPN. Kustok was getting her master's at DePaul in multicultural and corporate communications. They suggested to her she might want to see how television broadcasting works. She became a runner for the Big Ten Network's football telecasts, and the moment Kustok sat in a broadcast truck during a Michigan-Wisconsin game, she knew where her future lay. She started doing some high school games, then graduated to local television doing a number of odd jobs before she was hired by Comcast SportsNet in Chicago. She had the great pleasure of being the reporter the day White Sox pitcher Mark Buehrle threw a perfect game.

Then came the offer this one-time college basketball star could not refuse: the NBA and her current role as analyst for the Nets.

As with a number of my guests, I first encountered Sarah while reporting. She came on the scene, and you couldn't help but notice how attractive she was, but beauty is skin deep. Sarah was far more than a pretty face. She was talented and had an outgoing personality to match. She was diligent in her work preparation, and it was easy to see she wanted to succeed, although she wasn't pushy about it. On the contrary. Sarah was so likable, you wanted to see her succeed. We both covered the Blackhawks' first of three Stanley Cup championships in Philadelphia. It was an experience neither of us will ever forget. The Blackhawks won on a goal by Patrick Kane in overtime that disappeared into the net. No one knew it had gone in except Kane, who threw off his gloves in celebration and skated down the ice, where many of his teammates were still unsure he had scored. During this time, Sarah became more polished, and it was easy to see she was headed toward new heights. So it's no surprise she left Chicago in 2017 for New York and a chance to become the first female analyst for an NBA team.

There are two stories from this interview I want to focus on—one hilarious and one life-changing. First, the hilarious one.

It wasn't exactly a marriage proposal, but by the time it was over it certainly sounded like one. It didn't happen on some gorgeous island or with a plane flying overhead. No, this happened on a 200' by 85' sheet of ice! It was during the Shoot the Puck competition at the United Center, a popular feature between the second and third periods when three fans are chosen to shoot the puck from center ice into three small slots covering the net. Sometimes the group included celebrities or athletes. If they made it, they would get one chance at just one target at the other end of the ice for an even better prize.

"As the rink-side reporter for Comcast SportsNet, now NBC Sports Chicago, I would interview these individuals while they were shooting the puck," she remembered. "It was always an experiment with people being comfortable on television."

Little did Sarah realize what lay ahead one night during Shoot the Puck.

"At the end of one of the interviews, one of the fans they had selected from the crowd—I don't remember the words, I want to block this out—he expressed his love."

This is exactly the dialogue between the two: "I love it," declared the contestant. "Congrats!" exclaimed Sarah. "Thanks for being here."

And then the bombshell.

"I love you!" declared the contestant. "You're so pretty and beautiful, I love you."

Sarah replied, "I'm gonna say, thank you. Now I don't know what to say!"

"It was awkward," admitted the somewhat embarrassed Kustok during the podcast. "I don't know how they heard, but by the time I got to the dressing room to do the postgame interviews, all the guys in the locker room had seen it, heard about it. I got a healthy ribbing of being told I was loved and who I'm going to marry, and will you marry the guy? And God rest his soul, Steve Montador [he died in 2015] said during a one-on-one interview, 'How did Shoot the Puck go over tonight?'"

You could hear one player exclaiming, "Oh!" and others laughing.

"It was my best Shoot the Puck of the year!" she said.

Montador then said, "We clearly had an eventful dressing room. We've all been receiving emails and texts you're off the market, it appears. We want confirmation when the first date will be!"

So, of course, Kustok went along with this. "We're just jumping right in and getting married. It's a blind marriage."

Montador ended the madness with, "Good luck with that."

Kustok admitted that, when you do a Google search for her, this story comes up. It was a fun story at the time, one everyone, even Kustok, appreciated.

There is one story, however, Kustok found herself entangled with. One that had a profound and devastating effect.

While she was working in Chicago, her father, Allan, was accused of murdering his wife, Sarah's mother, Jeanie. Kustok had to testify at the trial, where she said she couldn't imagine her mother committed suicide, and at the same time saying she couldn't believe her father murdered her mother. Eventually, Allan Kustok was sentenced to 60 years in prison for the crime. The story gained national attention.

Kustok allowed herself a few moments to shed some light on that difficult time in her life. "The only thing I'll say about that, and it's not something I want to talk about publicly or get too deep into...the thing I think about, the thing someone told me early on is, a friend said, 'You will always be your mother's greatest legacy.'"

Kustok admitted she had great support from people in Chicago, including family and friends and those in the Chicago media who were her friends.

"I absolutely think about my mother and the angel she is, she was, and everything I am is because of her. That to me is my focus, that to me is my strength. That to me is how I find and protect my peace, and I'll continue to do that."

Kustok wasn't emotional during this segment. It was more a reflection and firm resolve in how she has been coping with this traumatic aspect of her life.

"As we know in this business and all professions that matter to people, the thing that matters to most to me is the person I am, how I treat people, so grateful to get to do what I do. But you never know how long this will last. We all know this a very subjective business. Some people may love you and some people may not, but the thing that matters most to me at the end of the day is, when you look in the mirror, what type of person are you? At the core of me, that's what I try to focus on, to maintain a strength and to maintain a peace."

Kustok has managed to do that while continuing to exhibit the great professional she is.

# Stacey King

HIS CATCHPHRASES have become legendary. "Gimme some hot sauce," "Sriracha," "Let me step back and kiss myself," "Mouse in the house, did you not get the memo," and "This is a man's game, no boys allowed."

And there's plenty more. King has turned himself into one of the most entertaining analysts in any sport. More often than not, he reduces his Chicago Bulls play-by-play man Adam Amin to uproarious laughter. The man is a walking encyclopedia of catchphrases. But King is also a deft analyst armed with great knowledge of the game and three championship rings, having played with Michael Jordan and Scottie Pippen on the Bulls' first threepeat. As a college athlete, King came out of Oklahoma with glittering stats and was the sixth overall pick in the 1989 draft. But he was reduced to mostly a bench player, what with the wealth of talent the Bulls had accumulated. King spent eight seasons in the NBA. He was also a coach, having spent three seasons in the CBA, in Sioux Falls and Rockford, leading the Rockford Lightning to a championship game.

King's broadcast career began in 2006, but his sense of humor began long before that. It was in 2008, when the Bulls selected Derrick Rose with the first pick in the draft, that King really sprouted as a broadcaster. Some of Rose's incredibly talented displays left King to utter, "Either get up or get out of the way." And then there was, "He just parted it like the Red Sea." And how about, "Big-time players make big-time plays"? And then there was King's signature, "Too big, too strong, too fast, too good."

King became a star behind the mic. This now rather bulky figure was one of the reasons you watched a Bulls game. And, man, can this guy talk. Which made our two-part interview even that more joyful.

Dealing with Stacey as a player was a joy, too, although I spent a lot more time interviewing Jordan, Pippen, John Paxson, and B.J. Armstrong. That said, Stacey understood the media's demands and delivered. As he's grown, King has become a go-to guy just to spend some time with. He's just as entertaining, but also a fount of knowledge about the game of basketball.

Now in his 17th season as a Bulls TV analyst, Stacey has become more critical, moaning at times the way the Bulls play defense. One particular situation was during a game against Cleveland in the 2022–23 season when the Bulls had a three-point lead with 4.4 seconds left. Donovan Mitchell, who was on his way to a 71-point performance, made the first of two free throws. Stacey pointed that out the Bulls needed to box out the lane in case Mitchell purposely missed the next free throw. The Bulls didn't, and Mitchell scored the game-tying basket. Stacey decried how he Bulls missed the assignment. As it turned out, the Cavaliers won the game in overtime, but the next day the league ruled Mitchell was in the lane before he missed the free throw. Didn't matter. The Bulls still lost, and Stacey had made his point.

As for his many catchphrases, Stacey said there's a fine line to all of that: "What I've learned over the years—and if you had asked me if I had been here this long, I wouldn't have believed you. When I stepped in, the great Johnny 'Red' Kerr, who I owe a lot of gratitude to, was the analyst. The Bulls took a person who didn't have any experience, and they put me next to a legend. I learned from Johnny for two years, and people got a chance early, like in 2006, to see a little bit of my personality as an analyst."

But as quick to remember, King went back to his playing days. "I was quick-witted as a player. I was always the one cutting up, having a good time, joking all the time, doing the Bill Cartwright voice."

Cartwright had a voice issue, so it sounded as if he had a mouthful of gravel. King will occasionally do the impression on the air, and you can't help but laugh.

"I was just keeping the team loose, and people remembered that. And so, as I go into broadcasting, I remember someone telling me, you can't be funny, you can't be animated, you gotta be professional and do it this way."

Wouldn't you like to know who this guy was?

"I said, scrap that. Why can't you have personality? Why can't be who you are? I made a promise to myself when I got drafted, the late, great Jerry Krause, who doesn't get the credit for being one of the greatest GMs of all time, gave me some advice when he drafted me. He said, 'Stacey, when you come here, you can't do that here. You've got to act like you've scored before and be the 21-year-old kid who listens to his boss.' I said, 'Okay, I'll change and I won't do that.'"

King was a top-notch player at Oklahoma and a flamboyant one, at that. He played with emotion and passion. One of the things he thrived on most was the energy of the crowd.

"When it was a big game, I rose to the challenge and everyone knew Stacey King was on the floor because of my antics. I emulated a lot of guys after they celebrated making a basket, and I put it in my game, and it took off. That made me the player that I was at the University of Oklahoma."

But those words from Krause didn't mesh with who King really was.

"I felt like that really took something from me as a player. It neutralized me. I didn't get up the same way I did in college. I didn't like it. It wasn't who I was."

King did understand why Krause wanted him to act differently. The Bulls were on the rise and didn't want any distractions. King accepted that role but...

"I told myself I would never let anyone take my personality from me again. And if you didn't like it, you shouldn't have drafted me. There were 29 other teams that could have drafted me and my personality, but I wanted rings! That was the sacrifice you make. I was on one of the greatest teams in NBA history. I played with two of the top players of all time, some great complementary players, great teammates, great Hall of Fame coach [Phil Jackson], Hall of

Fame assistant coaches, Hall of Fame GM. I wouldn't trade any of that for the world."

But that changed when King became a broadcaster. He promised himself he wouldn't let his personality be squelched or taken away from. King gives a lot of credit to the Reinsdorfs. Jerry had given the reins over to his son Michael.

"They've allowed me to be me. They've allowed me to grow into this fun, catchphrasing, nicknaming analyst. Now I see a lot of people doing what I do now. Back in 2007, you didn't see analysts calling games like I call games. So I'm a trendsetter!"

After working with play-by-play announcers like Tom Dore and Neil Funk, the Bulls eventually hired Adam Amin to fill the role. King is 6'11". Amin is 5'7". They appear to be a mismatch made in heaven.

"He's got a giant personality, which makes him about 6'8"! He's one of the bright young stars of broadcasting. I never thought we could replace Neil. Neil is a hall of famer. He had one of the most iconic voices. His personality really meshed well with me. Neil helped me be who I am today. He allowed me to do signature calls. Any signature call is usually done by the play-by-play guy. Neil allowed me to do that."

King admitted growing up in Lawton, Oklahoma, he was always a prankster.

"This is not a surprise to people who knew me as a kid. What they see now is what they saw when I was six, seven, eight years old."

Now King is in his mid-fifties and at the top of his game, which is another way of saying, "Too big, too strong, too fast, too good."

# HOCKEY

# Chris Chelios

WHAT'S THE first thing you think of when you hear the name Chris Chelios? Great Blackhawks defenseman? Chicago guy? Traitor? Big sports fan? Friend to the famous?

How about longevity?

Chelios played in the NHL for 26 years, until he was 48! Very few players have achieved such a lengthy career. Gordie Howe played until he was 52. Chelios was a smart and gritty player who won three Stanley Cups, two with the rival Detroit Red Wings and one with the Montreal Canadiens. He played in another Final with the Blackhawks. He was the first American-born player to captain a Montreal team, won three Norris Trophies as the league's best defenseman, played in a record 24 playoffs, and was elected to the Hockey Hall of Fame. He holds the distinction of playing for two Olympic teams, 22 years apart!

A native of Evergreen Park, a southwest suburb of Chicago, Chelios grew up a huge sports fan, something he remains to this day. He loved baseball, was too small for football, and didn't succeed at hockey until he joined a junior team in Canada. He was selected with the 40th overall pick by the Canadiens. From there, he joined fellow Chicagoan Eddie Olczyk on the 1984 Olympic team. Olczyk was selected third in the first round of that year's draft by the Blackhawks. Chelios spent seven years with Montreal and then, in a shocking trade, was sent to the Blackhawks for star center and future Hall of Famer Denis Savard. Chelios instantly became a fan favorite, but in 1999, the Blackhawks sent him to the hated Red Wings. Chelios was 38, but his career continued to thrive in the Motor City, where he helped the already potent Wings to two more championships.

Chelios left Detroit after the 2008–2009 season, played one season with the minor league Chicago Wolves, where he was called up briefly in 2010 to play for the NHL's Atlanta Thrashers. But after the season he finally retired at the age of 48.

But his hockey career isn't over. Not by a longshot.

Until June 2023, Chelios was a studio analyst for ESPN, but still works for the Blackhawks, who already employ his daughter, Caley, also a studio analyst for NBC Sports Chicago.

I first got to really know Cheli when he joined the Hawks in 1990. It was a tumultuous time, considering the volatile Mike Keenan was their head coach. They won the President's Cup for leading the league in points during the regular season, but were ousted in the first round of the playoffs. The team made the Stanley Cup Final the next season but were swept by Mario Lemieux, Jaromír Jágr, and the Pittsburgh Penguins.

Cheli was always available to the media. He was honest and forthright. As the years went by, Cheli was just as gracious while being a member of the Red Wings. "Detroit Sucks" may be the rally cry of Chicago sports fans, but Cheli was still one of theirs, even if he did hear a smattering of boos.

As I mentioned earlier, Cheli is one of the few athletes who played past the age of 45, so naturally, I wanted to get his impressions on some of the others who have endured lengthy and successful careers. But first, we started with why he played as long as he did, and was there ever a time he wanted to retire before he was 48.

"Closest I got was the end of my career in Chicago. I was 38, and things weren't going well with our team."

The Hawks finished out of the playoffs that season and the one before that.

"We struggled trying to make the playoffs, and I wasn't that guy who could play 30 minutes a game anymore or could carry a team. I was fortunate in Detroit. They had just won two Cups, and I fit in nicely. That's why I played so long. I didn't have to uproot my family for the last 10 years of my career. That had the most to do with it, being on a great team and, of course, staying relatively healthy and not suffering any significant injuries."

So, with that, we set our sights on Tom Brady, who completed his 23rd season at age 45, then retired.

"I don't think anyone wants to be the guy who takes out Tom Brady. He's got that luxury, and he's earned it, for sure. There's no question he takes care of himself. He's the first guy on the field and the last guy to leave."

Chelios considered Wayne Gretzky, who had teammates protect him on the ice. Brady had his offensive line, but the sport is more brutal than hockey.

"If it's me, and I'm playing against Brady, especially in the playoffs. First thing I'm going to do is take a 15-yard penalty on Brady and rattle him. But he's smart. He obviously doesn't put himself in real tough situations. If I look back, I always thought Michael Jordan was the greatest athlete ever. But I have to put Brady in there with him now, after what he's accomplished. Year in and year out, he just dominates and remains healthy."

Brady has been to the Super Bowl 10 times, winning seven. He finally retired after the 2022 season.

"I cheer for the old guys. I look at Zdeno Chára [who retired at 45 in his 24th season in the NHL], and it's amazing how a guy that size has managed to play as long as he did."

Speaking of age, Jaromír Jágr, now 51, stepped in to play for a team he owns in the Czech Republic in late December 2022. It means he won't be eligible for the Hockey Hall of Fame until 2026! Jágr played 24 seasons in the NHL, amassing 1,921 points. He's the league's fourth highest goal-scorer with 766!

"Ha! Unbelievable skill, but he bought his own team in Europe. That's pretty good, having the luxury of buying a team and then playing for that team. He was another kid, very serious in how he trained." (Remember, he broke in the season before the Penguins swept the Blackhawks to win the Stanley Cup in 1992.) "It's a different game over there. There's no hitting, you just got to play offense. Quite honestly, at 60, I can go play forward over there and get 10 goals a year. He obviously loves playing, so what? I'm sure the crowd loves watching him."

And then there's the ironman of ironmen, the incomparable Gordie Howe, who played until he was 52. As an aside, I ventured up to Detroit in 1980 as a freelance reporter to cover a game in which three Hall of Fame players were reunited on the then Hartford Whalers: Howe, Bobby Hull, and Dave Keon. I grew up watching them play, and then, as a 26-year-old reporter, had the pleasure of interviewing them.

Chelios remembered how effective Howe still was in his last season.

"I think he scored 20-something goals at age 52 [it was 15]. It's not like he was taking a spot. To score that many goals at that age is crazy. No one better than Gordie Howe, that's for sure. Gretzky's as good, but no one better than Howe."

Howe was also one of the league's strongest and most menacing players.

"He was a monster! For those years—late '50s, '60s, and early '70s—you looked at guys like Bobby Hull, Ted Lindsay, very small. Gordie, easily 6' and thick. He didn't fight a lot, but dirty as they come. Those elbows he was known for...looked like someone was going for him, and all of a sudden they're lying on the ice because Gordie stuck an elbow under their chin and knocked 'em out! He was a big, big guy for that time when he played."

Chelios wasn't a very big guy when he played, and while he lost more fights than he won, he was never shy to get into a scrap and was considered one of the league's toughest players. Now he gets to watch, rather than play.

Of course, there's always Jaromír Jágr's team, Cheli!

# Pat Foley

"HE SCORES!" Those two words were shouted often by the legendary Hockey Hall of Famer Pat Foley, who retired as the play-by-play announcer for the Chicago Blackhawks following the 2021–22 season. It capped a 41-year run in Chicago, including two with the minor league Wolves (after Foley was fired by the Blackhawks in 2006 and before being rehired in 2008). Foley was as much a part of the franchise as was their three Stanley Cup championships in the 2010s. His riveting voice combined with a pulsating delivery endeared him to Hawks fans not long after his arrival in 1980. Thanks to his father's automobile dealership and relationship with Michael Wirtz, a member of the family that has long owned and controlled the Blackhawks, Foley was hired and began the longest broadcast run in team history. His prominence rose dramatically just a few years after he was hired thanks to the emergence of Denis Savard and a team that became one of the league's most exciting during the 1980s. Unfortunately for the Hawks, Wayne Gretzky and the Edmonton Oilers stood in their way, and they were never able to make the Stanley Cup Final.

Foley also had the pleasure of working with top-notch analysts. His first was Dale Tallon, the sharp-witted former member of the team and later its general manager. He also worked with three other ex-Blackhawks: Bill Gardner; Troy Murray; and Eddie Olczyk, who also left the team after the 2021–22 season to take a similar job with the Seattle Kraken.

As synonymous as "He Scores!" was to Foley's announcing portfolio, his famous cry of "Bannerman!" after the goaltender made a great save in the 1980s is probably what he hears the most from fans and media.

Blessed with a boisterous laugh, Foley left an indelible mark on Chicago's broadcast scene. He's also an avid golfer who, now that he's retired, is playing as often as he can.

Pat came to town just a few years after I began my broadcasting career in Chicago. I would see him often at practices and in the dining hall, where he would sometimes get together with Bob Verdi, a revered writer who covered the Hawks, and share stories that had them laughing so hard the entire room could hear them. I would sit at their table from time to time and be left in tears. Pat is a gregarious sort who, at a retirement party for former longtime TV sportscaster Mark Giangreco, delivered a rollicking story that had a room full of journalists and friends laughing in delight. I would also visit him and Olczyk in their broadcast perch high above the United Center ice and allow them to berate me, albeit just for laughs. I can't tell you what a joy it was to hear his broadcasts. Pat and I were born just five days apart, and we're still both 39!

My interview with Pat also was the most unique of the more than the nearly 100 I have done. Because of an unforeseen circumstance, I invited him to do the interview from my dining room. He did, making this the most personal of all the podcasts and the only one not conducted via Zoom.

Of course, this had to be a two-part episode because of the myriad stories Pat told. One of them is a longer version of just how he landed the Blackhawks job through his father, Bob Foley. "We lost him a few years ago," Pat said, "and I said at the funeral, 'He's the reason I'm the voice of the Chicago Blackhawks.' He's the guy who drove me to Michigan State University after my sophomore year in high school, and in that trip, he set up a meeting with the head of the telecommunications department. I was able to meet this guy, and so when I applied to Michigan State, I got an early acceptance."

Good thing his father had some sway, because Foley admitted his grades weren't good enough to get into the university.

"I get through school, I get a couple of jobs professionally, and I apply for the Blackhawks job. Bill Wirtz's brother, Michael, bought his cars at Foley Buick. And Michael was a tough negotiator. He would dicker on price from now until next week, but once he bought his car, he maintained it meticulously."

Wirtz's dedication to maintaining his car would turn out to have an unexpectedly big impact on Pat Foley's career.

"So, when I applied for the Hawks job, Michael Wirtz eventually brings his car in for service. And guess what tape was in his cassette deck when he went home? He knew more about the Grand Rapids Owls than he wanted to know."

(The Owls were the team Foley covered in his previous gig.)

"My dad said, 'Mr. Wirtz, would you mind listening to this?' That helped me get the job, no question."

Foley took over when the Hawks were mediocre at best. They wound up in 10th and 14th place overall in Foley's first two years, respectively. Worse yet was the lack of radio rights.

"The Blackhawks were really having a hard time after Bobby Hull had left after the '72 season. They were in trouble with broadcasting rights because they were in the middle of a contract at the old WCFL, which is now WMVP-ESPN 1000. That station was sold, and they were a God squad. They were going 24 hours religion. They went to the Blackhawks in the middle of the summer and said, 'Yeah, we know we've got a contract with you, and we don't want you, so if you don't like it, sue us.'"

This is a very difficult predicament to be in, being one of the major sports franchises in town without a radio station, and having hired a guy the year before almost no one could hear.

"They had a guy, Andy McWilliams—'Whispering Andy.' McWilliams had lost his voice. They had the color guy [Bud Kelly] finish the 1979-80 season. They got no broadcaster, and they got no station, so I better let them know I'm around. I sent my stuff in, and by the way, the Grand Rapids Owls folded that season, so I need a job! I let the Hawks know I'm around, but I apply to other minor league teams. I get an offer from the Erie Blades."

The Blades were run by Nick Polano, who later built the Detroit Red Wings into Stanley Cup champions by bringing in five Russian players.

"Now it's getting into September, and I haven't heard from the Hawks. Nick calls me and says, 'Training camp starts in a week, what are we doing?' I said, 'Nick, will you give me one more day?' He did, so I called a certain person in the Blackhawks and said, 'I know you can't promise me anything, but do I have a shot at this job?' The answer was, 'Yes you do. We don't know where this is going to go, but you do have a shot.'"

Talk about hanging like a piece of tape off a used hockey stick.

"Here I am, 26 years old, and I call Nick Polano the next day and say, 'Thanks for waiting, but I have a shot at the NHL, so I'm going to take it.' So I'm either in the NHL that season, or I'm out of hockey. I got the job, and nobody remembers this: the start of the '80 season, the first five games of the year were not broadcast. They didn't have a radio station! So they make a deal with WYEN, an FM station [located in suburban Des Plaines]. In the Chicago Stadium, you couldn't hear WYEN. And I got a call from Bill Wirtz's secretary before Game 3 of that season. She said, 'Mr. Wirtz wants to see you tomorrow night.' I go down there and make a deal, so my first game was Game 6 of the season, which is the night they retired Stan Mikita's jersey [Mikita eventually was elected to the Hockey Hall of Fame]. Nobody's probably alive to remember, those first five games weren't on radio."

No, but many do remember when Foley was fired after the 2005–2006 season.

"There were a couple of people in the Blackhawks who were after me for a decade plus. They wanted me out. Rocky Wirtz [one of Bill's sons] told me in his dad's later years he felt that maybe dementia was setting in. Bill knew Chicago like the back of his hand, but he was getting lost going home. I don't know if that had anything to do with my dismissal, but that season the Hawks were breaking up their simulcast. It never got that far, and they fired me."

That's when Don Levin, owner of the minor league Wolves and an astute businessman, hired Foley to work alongside Bill Gardner. But it didn't happen without some luck.

"Mark Cuban had a network or television station that did a game of the week. I got a hold of this guy who told me he can't hire me because Cuban had a mandate to hire a nobody."

This is when the wheels in Foley's head started to turn, and turn fast. He knew Judd Sirott was doing the Wolves games, so he told him about Cuban's NHL game of the week. Sirott took the job, and that's how Foley wound up with the Wolves. Sirott eventually landed his own NHL gig with the Boston Bruins.

Two years later, Foley was back with the Blackhawks. So one Wirtz (Bill) fired him, and another Wirtz (Rocky), now chairman of the Hawks, hired him back. Foley quipped, "I'm quite proud of the fact I changed jobs twice and still live in the house I bought in 1984! I'm a Glenview guy, and it never works in this way, when you get into the business and you wind up working in your home town."

Foley came out of retirement for one game, an outdoor contest at Fenway Park. He broadcast the game for Sports USA.

# Eddie Olczyk

HE'S A native of Chicago, played on the US Olympic team, was drafted by and played for his hometown team (the Blackhawks), once coached an NHL team, and became one of the game's leading analysts. Eddie Olczyk's life would appear to be a dream come true, and it is, save for a battle with colon cancer, a celebrated battle he won. Now an analyst for the Seattle Kraken, as well as TNT, Olczyk continues to evolve. After being the lead analyst for the Blackhawks for 16 years, alongside Hall of Famer and now retired Pat Foley for all but two of them, Olczyk couldn't negotiate a new contract, so he left for Seattle, where his brother is the assistant GM and two of his sons are also with the organization.

Olczyk joined the Blackhawks as their first-round pick in 1984. He spent three seasons with them, scoring 65 goals, but then was traded to Toronto. Olczyk would eventually play for six teams over a 16-year career, but spent his last two back in Chicago. In 2003 Olczyk was named head coach of the Pittsburgh Penguins, where he languished for a season and a half, winning only 27 percent of his games. A year later, Olczyk began his broadcast career. He called three Blackhawks Stanley Cup championships, working beside the incomparable Doc Emrick. He also hosted many events, including the retirement of Marian Hossa's jersey, this while being the voice of the Kraken. Olczyk is also a horse racing expert who was hired by NBC to be part of its triple crown coverage.

I was a reporter covering a lot of hockey games when I first met Eddie. I got the sense that he would be more than just a very good hockey player. This guy could talk! I kiddingly told several of my cohorts in the industry he was going to take our jobs. You could tell Eddie not only loved to play, he loved the lights, cameras, and microphones. And Eddie was very accessible, which made him even more popular and important to the fourth estate.

There is another thing or two that endears Eddie to just about everyone he comes in contact with: a vibrant personality and knowledge of the sport—not only the rules, but strategy and how a team can be put together. Eddie readily admitted he wanted to become general manager of a team, having interviewed several times, but never the team he wanted a closer association with—the Blackhawks.

On top of all that, Eddie is a fabulous storyteller and does so with panache. He was one of my first interviews, two months before the podcast debuted, and he was good as any of the nearly 100 I've done. This particular story was told with such detail, recall, and humor that I simply have to share it with you.

"This one takes the cake," a giggling Olczyk began. "Everybody in sports gets traded or fired. We all know that. People get released, people get terminated."

In this case, Olczyk was referring to the second time in his NHL career that he got traded.

"It was November 9, 1990. It was an off-day in Toronto [where Olczyk had landed after the Blackhawks], and oddly enough we were going to play the Blackhawks, Saturday night, *Hockey Night in Canada*. And my wife, Diana, was very pregnant, and her water broke on the 9th. I called our PR man and told him I wouldn't be at the morning skate, but I [was] going to be at the game."

His wife, of course, was going into labor.

"Just letting the coaches know I'll be at the game tomorrow night. So, of course, Diana is not cooperating, and the next morning she's still not cooperating, meaning on a scale of 1 to 10 she was about a 1½ or 2. But I said, it's an 8:00 o'clock game, we've got 12 hours, and I can get to Maple Leaf Gardens in a matter of about a half hour."

The plot thickens.

"About 11:30, I call the Maple Leafs to let them know, hey, Diana hasn't had the baby yet, but I'm gonna be at the game. At about 2:30, 3:00 o'clock, Diana starts cooperating. And the doctor says, 'Let me put on my catcher's mitt, we're gonna have ourselves a baby.'

"'Okay, doc, let's go, I've got a hockey game to go to.' That's was pretty much what I was thinking about. While we're in labor, at about 5:00 o'clock, a nurse taps me on the shoulder and hands me a note."

The plot thickens even further.

"All it says is, 'The Maple Leafs are on the phone.' I look at my wife, she's on her back and about to have a baby. The doctor is at the foot of the bed. There's medical equipment everywhere, and there are people all over the place. I tell the nurse, 'Tell the Leafs I will be at the game, Diana's having the baby.' She leaves. She might have been gone 90 seconds and says, 'They really want to talk to you.' What do I do, George? What do I do at that particular stage? Do I sit there and take the call or do I continue to support my wife on giving birth to our second child?"

Such a conundrum! I asked Eddie whether he had any inkling why the Leafs were so adamant about him taking the call. "I have no idea. I think they're calling to just check in with my wife. 'Hey, take the night off, we'll get through without you.' That's what I was thinking."

That's not exactly what the Leafs were thinking.

"Monty Hall, *Let's Make a Deal*. I say, 'Oh, screw it, I'm going to take the call.'" Olczyk is giggling through all of this. "So I try to sneak out of the room, and my wife says, 'Where are you going?'

"'Ahhh, I got to take a phone call.' I go to the nurse's station and get on the phone, and it's Bob Stellick, the PR guy. He says, 'Hey, Eddie, how's Diana?'"

This is not what Eddie wants to hear. He's somewhat perturbed.

"'She's having the baby, I'm gonna be at the game.' He said, 'Call us after she's had the baby.' I said Bob, 'I'm not calling. I'll be at the game. I'm gonna play.'"

This was when Eddie, Diana, and their family's life was about to change.

"Then there's an awkward pause, and all Bob says is, 'Hold on a second,' and I'm like, 'She's having the baby,' and he says, 'Hold on.' The general manager of the Maple Leafs is on the other line. It's Floyd Smith. He goes, 'Eddie, we hate to do this to you right now.'"

Eddie is really chuckling now.

"'We hate to do this to you now, but I have to inform you, by league rules, we've just traded you to the Winnipeg Jets.'"

You can imagine what was going through Eddie's head.

"My heart stopped, and I was like, 'You gotta be bleeping me! You gotta be kidding. You just traded me while my wife is in the delivery room giving birth to our child, and you have the balls to tell me I just got traded?'

"I said, 'Just forget about it,' and I hung up the phone. I'm stunned now. I'm standing at the nursing station, saying what do I do? Most people would say, 'Get your ass back in the delivery room where you have the baby with your wife!'"

This is not what Eddie did first.

"I get on the phone and call my dad and tell him I was traded. I wander back into the delivery room, and it's maybe five minutes since the time I left, and again I'll paint the picture: doctor's in the room, nurses in the room, medical contraptions everywhere, and the lovely and talented Diana Olczyk on her back getting ready to give birth. She sees me walk in and says, 'Where in the hell have you been?'"

This is where Eddie has to become creative.

"'Ah, my aunt's sick.' She looks at the ceiling and she looks back at me, and I swear on my last breath she says, 'Where are we going?'"

If you're thinking in terms of woman's intuition, you are correct!

I said, "She knew, she knew."

Eddie came back, "I said to myself, 'Psychic and pregnant!'"

I burst out laughing, and Eddie was laughing too, while trying to navigate this hilarious tale.

"Now I take a look at the doctor at the foot of the bed, and he's got this look on his face like, 'How are you gonna get yourself out of this one, Olczyk?' So, I say to Diana, 'Guess?' And again, I swear on my last breath she says Winnipeg! And I go, 'Oh...my...God!' How in the hell did she know? I'm shaking my head, she's shaking her head, and then I look at the head of the bed, and the doctor is pulling off his rubber gloves and going, 'This baby is not going to be born for a while.'"

We both can't stop laughing. The story is so good it can't be true, but it is.

"About two and a half hours later, Thomas Vincent Olczyk came into this world, and I had a chance to be with Tommy and Diana that night."

Eddie got on a plane the next morning and ironically flew to Chicago and played his first game with the Jets. Then he flew back to Toronto and oddly enough, the Jets were playing in Toronto that night. "Eventually, they joined me in Winnipeg, six weeks later," Eddie said.

Eddie spent two and a half seasons with the Jets before they traded him to the New York Rangers, where he won a Stanley Cup. Then the Rangers traded Eddie back to Winnipeg, who less than two seasons later traded him to the Los Angeles Kings. One season later, it was on to Pittsburgh for a small part of one season and another full one before he finally returned to the Blackhawks. During that time, the Olczyks had another son and a daughter.

One more thought: I don't bet on sporting events as rule, except for one, the Kentucky Derby. And many times I have asked Eddie for his best long-shot Trifecta pick, and then I bet it. So far, he's come close, but I haven't cashed in yet.

I'm waiting, Eddie!

# JOURNALISTS / MEDIA PERSONALITIES

# Peggy Kusinski

SHE'S BOLD, spirited, a foodie, and a wine geek. And she happens to be a darn good sports reporter and commentator. Peggy Kusinski has established herself as one of Chicago's premier sportscasters, who took her love of sports as a youth and transformed it into a very successful career. Now a weekend cohost with ABC-7's Dionne Miller and postgame host on Bears broadcasts on WMVP Radio, Kusinksi has redefined herself. She started her career in radio, moved to television in 1996, and became an award-winning anchor and reporter on WMAQ-TV for 16 years. But as she stepped back from her television role, Kusinski decided to develop a podcast with one of her sons, aptly titled *The Sportscaster and Her Son*. A native Chicagoan and one of nine siblings, Kusinski grew up with seven brothers. No wonder she liked sports! It started early, when her father worked as a janitor at Elmwood Park High School. She would go there on weekends and spend time in the gym shooting baskets. She tried out for her sixth-grade team in grammar school, but the coach said, "This is the boys' team, the girl's tryouts aren't until seventh grade." Kusinksi's mom told her to go back and tell the coach she wanted to try out for the boys' team. Her mom played basketball in high school. Kusinski eventually played on the girls' team and added volleyball and 16″ softball. Sports was everything to her. It would translate in a different way when she attended Southern Illinois University, where I got my training as a sportscaster. But it began with being a standup comic. There was a search HBO was doing for standup comics, and Kusinksi tried it twice. She finished second in a competition, but when she told her mother of this venture, the response was a rather firm, "Over my dead body!"

While at SIU, Kusinski walked into one of her brother's apartments and saw Gayle Gardner doing *SportsCenter* on ESPN. That's when the light went on. She couldn't believe a woman was doing sports. She went back to the radio and TV department and signed up. From there, a career blossomed. Kusinski would find her way to WMAQ radio, where she was the first woman to host a sports talk show called *The Sports Huddle*. After stints as a producer for the 1992 summer and winter Olympic Games, she returned to ply her trade on TV as an anchor and host. Then it was on to WMAQ and a sterling career that continues today back on ESPN 1000.

Having already been in the business for some 10-plus years, I met Peggy covering games and events. She wasn't shy, a trait I really admired. She became just another member of the media mob and not a woman trying to blaze a trail along with Cheryl Raye-Stout, another guest on my podcast. She delivered tough questions but also sprinkled in a sense of humor. It seemed like anywhere I went, Peggy was there, tirelessly plying her trade. It's one of the reasons she received six local Emmy awards for her work. Chicago is a very competitive market, and Peggy fit right in.

What I really liked about my interview with Peggy was her honestly and vulnerability. She was upfront with her feelings on a number of topics, and her emotions ranged from joy, frustration, and embarrassment to disappointment and relief. Our conversation was a hit right off the bat because we discussed mutual interests: food and wine.

"I cry when Michelin-star chefs cook for me," Kusinski declared with outright devotion. "When my husband and I travel around the world, our dinner revolves around the Michelin Guide."

The Michelin Guides are a revered and respected series of books published by the eponymous French tire company that awards restaurants around the world up to three stars for excellence.

"We collect pictures of menus and great chefs and have them framed in my kitchen."

You kind of get the idea. Peggy likes food.

"I appreciate the chef's talent and artistic vision." But Peggy also loves wine. "I fully admit to being a wine snob, and during the pandemic I took the Level 1 wine course." Level 1 is the entry level to being a sommelier.

But first and foremost, we talked about her career as a sports-caster, which took a difficult turn in 2015.

"I was mailing it in with my job. When I was in radio, I hated all those people who would complain. If you don't like it, get out! I found myself in television starting to complain. But when I really self-reflected, the life-altering moment was when my sister died. She was in her 11th year battling breast cancer, and I took time out to take care of her. I had the full support of management at WMAQ-TV. They would allow me to cover Bulls or Bears practice in the northern suburbs. I would do my stories quickly, hand them over to my cameraman, and then go to my sister's house and take care of her."

This went on for a grueling seven months before she died.

"It made me reflect. I had covered three Bulls championships, three Blackhawks Stanley Cups, the Bears in the Super Bowl, and the White Sox and Cubs World Series titles. But I had been thinking about it for the last two years. What am I doing here? What else am I waiting for?"

Peggy had missed so many Christmases, Thanksgivings, T-ball games, and other activities involving her sons and daughter.

"One time during the Stanley Cup in Tampa, I covered practice, flew home to watch my daughter's dance recital, got a flat tire, got someone to help me fix it, made the recital, raced back to the airport, and got back in time during the national anthem. This is what I was doing to try to do everything!"

It took a toll on Peggy. She was emotionally spent. This led to one of her most embarrassing moments. It happened after former Blackhawks star Patrick Kane scored a winning goal during a playoff game. "I asked Kane if this was the first overtime goal game-winner? He looked at me out of the corner of his eye but didn't call me out. I could see some of the smirks from some of the Blackhawks beat writers, and I was pissed. Why are they looking at me like that?"

Peggy didn't realize the gaffe she'd made. We've all been there before. Everyone's looking at you, willing to offer you a shovel so you can dig yourself out of an embarrassing hole. It's a lonely, unforgiving place to be. "When I was driving home, I heard on a national radio show...'What an idiot, what a dingbat. She must not know hockey.' I was so stunned. It hit me what I had done."

But it didn't get any better for Peggy.

"I think sometimes for women we are so ultra-conservative about getting it right and not making a mistake. I couldn't sleep that night. My son said, 'Mom, you're all over Twitter.' And I said, 'Oh, no!' It was heartbreaking, some of the comments said about me."

The next morning, Peggy drove to the airport hangar where the Blackhawks leave for road trips. The PR guy for the Blackhawks approached her. "He pulled me aside and said, 'Are you okay?' I was fighting back tears. I said, 'I'm just not myself these days. My sister died three weeks ago. I just screwed up.' He said, 'Don't worry, we all have your back.'"

But while she was driving to St. Louis to cover the game, Peggy turned on the radio, something she probably regrets doing. "It was all over the radio. It was terrible. I got to the hotel and I cried and cried. I had a breakdown in the hotel, and I think it was all the tears because of my sister. I called a reporter friend of mine. He told me to let it go, but that led to my final decision. I was done and deciding to step away."

But Peggy is back. While she continues to do her podcast with her son, her Saturday show on ESPN 1000 with Dionne Miller has become a big hit. She's also covering the Bears, doing a postgame show with John Jurkovic, who does a weekday show on the station with Carmen DeFalco.

I don't know if Peggy has taken the second test toward becoming a sommelier, but I do know she's in a much better place, and sports fans here are in a better place because of that.

# Corey McPherrin

TRANSITION. Sometimes we want to, and sometimes we have to. In the media business, it happens often. People go from company to company and sometimes in different roles. Corey McPherrin did it, only he didn't change companies. Instead, the longtime veteran sports anchor and reporter switched to news. It happened in 2010, some 15 years after he joined WFLD-Fox 32 in Chicago. The extremely affable McPherrin actually began his sports broadcasting career in 1977 in Davenport, Iowa. And then, like a ship making ports of call, McPherrin earned jobs in Quincy, Illinois; New Orleans; Denver; and New York before coming to Chicago in 1991. McPherrin's journey allowed him to grow and offered him some very tantalizing stories, but after 33 years, he was promoted to host of *Good Day Chicago* on Fox 32. McPherrin joined the likes of Tim Weigel, Ryan Baker, and national notables such as Keith Olbermann in making the change. McPherrin has been thriving since, though he admitted he does miss sports.

A native of Chicago, McPherrin couldn't resist an opportunity to come home, which is why he left a very plum job with WABC in New York. His son Jack had just been born, and McPherrin declared, "I don't want him growing up a Yankees fan."

So he returned to his roots.

As with most people who are featured in this book, I met Corey on the beat, and he was instantly likable. And I knew from the start he was a consummate pro. He never tried to be adversarial or controversial. He is one of the very good guys in our business. There was always a smile on his face, yet a determination to get his story and get it right. I also made occasional appearances on a Sunday night show he hosted called *The Final Word*, which included former

Bears wide receiver Tom Waddle. We would tackle three questions in a short span with Corey pairing the two of us. It was quick, witty, and a joy to do, and part of the reason was because of Corey's friendly delivery.

McPherrin covered many stories and personalities during his time in the sports world, and he tells of two instances—one in which he was with dealing with a breaking story, and one in which he was dealing with someone who was used to breaking people.

The first was in 1989, when McPherrin was covering the Bay Bridge World Series between the San Francisco Giants and the Oakland Athletics, an earth-shattering Series to say the least.

"ABC had the World Series at that time," he recalled, "and we, as the ABC station in New York, got to go out there and cover it. They thought it was a neat thing to do, and we would have coverage before and after the game and to a huge audience."

*Huge* would turn out to be an understatement.

"What I remember most about it was the night before the earthquake, a lot of us had gone out, as one is wont to do at a certain age on the road with fellow broadcasters, and had a few libations. I remember getting in late, and all I remember the next day was thinking, *I wished I hadn't stay out so late, I'm really tired. I can't wait to get back to the hotel and get to bed.*"

Well, it certainly turned out to be the longest day and night in McPherrin's professional life. The earthquake struck just before the start of the game at Candlestick Park.

"I had just done my live shot back to New York, and I look out at the parking lot, and the first thing I see—the light poles out there—and I'm saying, why are the light poles moving? And why does the parking lot look like it's waving? And I'm saying, I do I not feel well. Why am I not seeing this thing right?"

The earthquake struck with a vengeance, and only a few in the park knew the gravity of the situation.

"You look up and turn around, and straight up the light standards arc moving! And then I'm in this big satellite truck, and it must be thousands of pounds, and it's wobbling!"

McPherrin's voice goes up an octave, as if he's reliving the moment right then and there.

"And, oddly enough, I'm on the phone with Tim Weigel [who was working at Channel 7, the ABC affiliate in Chicago] because I had done a live shot for Chicago. I was helping out other ABC stations that day. And I said, 'Timmy, I got to hang up,' and somebody who knew L.A. said, 'This is an earthquake.' This all happened in like 14 seconds."

The players walked out of their respective dugouts with family trying to join them, and they eventually took off in their cars. They had no idea what awaited them, what with the Bay Bridge out and numerous fires taking place across the city of San Francisco.

"We covered the heck out of that thing all night, and the next morning we were on the Regis and Kathie show, and we fed it back to the morning news show in New York. And the real *coup de grâce* for me—and I'll never forget, I was so tired—the next morning, I'm sort of dismissed for a while to go back to the hotel to get a few hours of sleep."

This is when McPherrin had another one of those life-altering moments.

"Right in front of me, coming the other way is ABC News anchor Peter Jennings, who I never met. He knew me enough as we passed, he said, 'Nice job, kid.' And I couldn't believe it. The fact he even recognized me. But the night before, he apparently had seen what I had done. And that was the finest compliment I ever got. I'll never forget it."

Jennings was the preeminent anchor of his time—a very polished journalist with outstanding reporting skills who transformed into an exceptionally smooth and articulate anchor. He commanded every topic presented him with great aplomb.

But Jennings wasn't the only famous figure McPherrin has dealt with. There was also one of the most menacing figures of his time, boxer Mike Tyson.

"He was living about an hour and a half north of New York City. So we go up there, having somehow managed to get through to him.

He had just won a couple of fights and was gaining some notoriety. So we go up there and capture him on his farm, where he lived with [trainer] Cus D'Amato and his family. We get to know him a bit, and he shows us these pigeons. He was from Brooklyn, and he was very raw and very young, but one of the questions he asked me, 'Hey, ah, what do you do...I'm 19, and I can't rent a car. How do I do that? And these girls keep coming up to me, and they want to get together, and I don't know what I should do.'"

This left McPherrin incredulous. He figured he might as well be Ann Landers!

"I'm 29, 30 years old. I'm not much older than him! So, I'm trying to give him some advice and thinking, *What am I doing here with this kid?*"

Too bad McPherrin couldn't offer some advice on biting off an ear!

# Dave Revsine

DAVE REVSINE is the very popular host and play-by-play voice for the Big Ten Network. As a matter of fact, he was the original host when the network debuted in late August 2007. It was a big leap of faith for Revsine, who was an anchor at ESPN the previous 10 years. But after receiving his fourth contract with a minimal raise, Revsine felt the time was right to look elsewhere. The Big Ten Network targeted Revsine as their main guy, and in 2007 he was hired to be its studio host.

Revsine, who grew up in suburban Chicago and attended Northwestern University, began his broadcast career on its campus radio station. But his first real job was as an investment banker in New York, a job he didn't care for. It was then on to the tiny town of Sherman, Texas, where he was hired as a TV sportscaster after having his résumé rejected over 100 times! Then Revsine moved on to the Quad Cities before landing at ESPN, where the network had a bevy of stars like Keith Olbermann, Dan Patrick, and Charley Steiner, to name a few.

Revsine also wrote a critically acclaimed book in 2014, *The Opening Kickoff: The Tumultuous Birth of a Football Nation*, which made the *New York Times* bestseller list—which had also been rejected by many publishing houses.

While I've never met Dave in person, we both knew of each other's work, and he was a listener to my podcast, which made our first meeting a very successful one. And it was Dave who suggested I interview Lisa Byington, the voice of both the Milwaukee Bucks and the Chicago Sky of the WNBA, which I did.

Dave is a tremendous storyteller. He injects such enthusiasm in every one of them, so here are just two. The first was about his early days at ESPN and the second, an eye-opening encounter with a notorious figure.

"It was 1996, and I was 27 years old," Revsine began. "I was only in the business for three years, so in some ways I got to ESPN rather quickly, although there were certainly a lot of people who never thought I would get there...based on their reactions to my résumé tape. So I had gone from being a weekend anchor at the worst station in the Quad Cities to ESPN. I was one of the original hires when the network launched ESPN News."

Among those original hires were also Mike Greenberg, Chuck Garfien, John Buccigross, and Michael Kim.

"A couple weeks in, they invite us to an all-staff meeting. Here I am, just removed from the 88th market in the country, and I'm sitting in the same room with Keith Olbermann, Dan Patrick, Chris Berman, Mike Tirico, and Chris Fowler, and all of these people, some of whom I idolized growing up, and now. In a weird sort of way, I'm one of their colleagues.

"The meeting gets started, and at the end, they open it up to some questions. And Keith, who is at the height of his powers—I mean, he and Dan, the *Sunday Big Show*, is the biggest thing going at the network. And Keith raises his hand and starts up on some of his issues. He starts complaining about the loudspeaker system. It was right above his desk, and it was giving him a headache.

"Olbermann was never enamored of management, nor they, of him. So they tell him he's the only one with such a complaint and if he can find some other people with a similar issue they might consider this complaint.

"I had been there some 20 minutes, and suddenly I feel this presence hovering over me.... I look up and it's Keith. He looks at me and says, 'Which one are you?' I say, 'Keith, I'm Dave Revsine, and I really respect your work.' And he says. 'I knew you were at this meeting, and this loudspeaker is really bothering me. They said If I can get a petition going they might consider it, so here's a petition, you want to sign it?'"

Talk about being in a tough place. Revsine is the new kid on the block and one of his idols is asking him to sign a petition.

"Here's one of my idols. And, as it turns out, he was very helpful in a couple of junctures in my career. Of course, I knew none of this at the time. All I knew was he was under management's skin, and that was the last place I wanted to get. So I said to him, 'At this stage of my career, I don't think it's a good idea [that] I sign this petition. I hope you'll understand.' And he was great. He laughed and he said, 'I get it. Nice to meet you,' and walked away. And that was the end of it."

The second story is one of those that is rather hard to believe. It started innocently, as part of a vacation with his family in Martha's Vineyard. It was the summer of 2003, and Dave was living in Connecticut, as he was working for ESPN at the time.

"I vacillate telling you this story," said Dave, now ready to spill the beans. "I'm not proud of this. We went for a week's vacation and rented a house there, and I was able to negotiate [with my wife] to play golf. She was great. We had a young kid, and this was her vacation, too. She said, 'Go play golf one time. Knock yourself out.'"

This was comforting news for Dave, who likes playing golf, only he had no idea of what lay ahead.

"I contact Farm Neck, which is the really famous golf course on Martha's Vineyard, where Bill Clinton and Barack Obama played. It's a private course in the morning and a public course in the afternoon. So I call for a tee time, and I'm a single, and they said, 'Yeah, we got a tee time at 2:00 o'clock, so why don't you come out? We got a threesome, so you can join them.'"

Dave readily agreed. He would get that one round of golf in that would put a punctuation mark on his vacation.

"I go out there, and I'm on the range and hitting balls, and I'm not hitting them well. I'm stressed out. It's maybe 1:52, and I look at my watch and I say, 'I gotta go.'"

Dave got in his cart and sped over to the 1st tee. "There are two carts there, one with two bags and the other with one, and the starter says, 'Put your bag on the cart with one. Those guys went in to get bug spray, and they're coming right out.'"

Dave's anticipation is building. Who are these guys, and who is he paired with?

"I'm working on my swing, and they come out, and I'm not paying attention, I'm looking down. And the first guy says his name, and I say, 'Hi, I'm Dave.' And the second guy says his name, and I say, 'Hi, I'm Dave,' and the third guy says, 'I'm O.J.'"

O.J. Simpson. It was *the* O.J. Simpson.

"And I look up at him, and I [think], *Oh, my goodness. What am I supposed to do, think about this?* So, at this point, it's 1:58. We're teeing off in two minutes. This is the one round of golf I negotiated. I am at this point a public figure."

Dave notes that while he's working at ESPN-TV, he shouldn't be unknown to O.J.

"But I'm a public figure, what am I supposed to do? Am I supposed to go with this guy? I really want to play golf." Dave chuckles and continues. "But this doesn't seem like a great idea. And in that moment...we just teed off. And the crazy thing was, I get in the cart and I sit down, and O.J. sits next to me. So we have a threesome, and they put O.J. with someone he doesn't know!"

As Dave put it, what would you do?

"So at 1:57 I'm thinking to myself, *Who am I playing golf with?* And at 2:02 I'm hurtling down the first fairway with O.J. Simpson! It was crazy.... Yeah, it ended up being a really weird day. And, look, my joke afterward—I kept trying to think of quips in my head—well, obviously he's going to quit after nine to continue to search for the real killer."

We were both laughing at this rather clever though sinister remark.

"No way this guy's got time for 18, right? But, look, he was very solicitous, trying to convert America, one golfer at a time, to be on his side. So what are you supposed to do? He asked what I did for a living, and I said I was an accountant. He apparently didn't watch enough of ESPN to know who I was or frankly didn't care, and yeah, that was the end of it. But I will say, at the end of it, I said, 'I'm going to turn in this score with my handicap. Will you mind attesting this on the scorecard?'"

This might have been one of the more transparent things anyone has done.

"So I got him to sign the scorecard, which I still have. And then, I was still really paranoid. It was a bad decision. I mean, in hindsight, if I was presented the same spot today, I wouldn't play. I wouldn't lie to him. But at the time I did. I was a little nervous about it, only told a couple of people, and I said, 'Don't tell anyone.' And that was it. My round with O.J."

I wonder if Dave told his wife, and whether he was ever able to negotiate a round of golf again.

# Cheryl Raye-Stout

IMAGINE BEING nicknamed "The Straw That Stirs the Drink." The title was bestowed on Cheryl Raye-Stout by the late Chet Coppock, longtime sportscaster in Chicago. It happened on her very first day on the job when she was named producer for Coppock's nighttime radio sports talk show titled *Coppock on Sports*. That was 1984, and Coppock wasn't pleased by the move. Raye-Stout says he heard him say on the phone to someone, "They hired some broad for me." So, in order to convince Coppock she wasn't "some broad," she decided to go big on her very first day and managed to get then Cubs general manager Dallas Green as a guest. And from that very first show, Coppock decided to call Raye-Stout "The Straw That Stirs the Drink."

Raye-Stout had already begun her career at WMAQ radio a few years earlier, but her first real sports job was as Coppock's producer. In the interim, she became the first woman to carry a microphone and recorder into a locker room and the first to do a sports talk show. She began getting phone numbers from everyone she met. But she was met with some resistance by athletes who weren't ready to see a woman in their locker room. She thanks Tony La Russa for helping smooth that road during his first stint as White Sox manager.

Raye-Stout went on to work for WMVP in Chicago, and for the last 20-plus years, she's been reporting sports for WBEZ, the NPR affiliate in Chicago.

I've known Cheryl about as long as anyone in the business, and to be honest with you, she quickly became "one of the guys" in the press box. Cheryl isn't a wallflower. She would ask questions to managers and players, never shying away from the job at hand. And since many of us covered a bunch of games back in the 1980s,

1990s, and 2000s, we got to see a lot of each other. The electronic media was shunned early on by some members of the print media, but we managed to more than prove our abilities and professionalism. Cheryl had it even tougher because she was a woman, and yet here she is now, still reporting on games and practices while much of the radio media has shrunk considerably. She told me there are many times when she's the only one in the press box!

Cheryl has broken her share of stories during her career, but none were bigger than these two, both involving one of the most famous athletes in the world, Michael Jordan.

"Michael and I had a great rapport, which you could have with a player. Back in the day, Michael would talk before games, he would talk after games, he would talk after practices. He talked all the time. He was very accessible, and I would go to night practices to talk to him when other people didn't bother to go. And also I was one of the few reporters covering the other teams, so I knew the White Sox really well."

This came in handy in a way Raye-Stout couldn't have imagined. Jordan had just retired from the Bulls after their third championship in 1993.

"His father had been murdered that summer. It was October 5, and he was going to throw out the first pitch before a Sox playoff game—but scroll back about a year and a half. I had a conversation with Michael before a game, and we were talking about baseball. He had taken some batting practice at the old Comiskey Park. He said to me, 'You really love baseball,' and I said, 'Yeah.' He said to me, 'One of these days, I'll play baseball.' And I said, 'By the time you retire, you don't want to ride the buses.'"

Scroll forward and return to 1993.

"I had this source that worked for the Cubs, and he said to me, 'Michael is going to play for the White Sox.' I said, 'Really?' He said, 'I can't tell you any more than that. You have to work it on your own.'"

Talk about a tip!

"I told my sports director at WMVP, 'I've got this story. I'm gonna work on it, but I'm going to get this story.' I made calls. And

I had a friend who was working security for the White Sox, and I called her up on a whim and I said, 'What time does Michael get there to work out?' and she said about 10:00...' And then she stops and says, 'You don't really know, do you?' I said, 'You just confirmed it for me!'"

Now that's the way to get a story. It was a very satisfying moment for Raye-Stout.

"It was, and it was exciting. But you had to be very careful because, if you messed up, you're talking about your credibility, your integrity with *the* sports figure in America."

So, like a good reporter, Raye-Stout made sure she had more than one source. She wound up confirming it with then trainer Herm Schneider and then White Sox general manager Ron Schueler. But a wrinkle developed.

"Somebody called the The Score [the other sports radio station and first ever in Chicago] and said they saw Michael going into Comiskey Park. So my sports director called and said we just heard the same thing and we have to break the story now because you have all the pieces there. So we broke the story, but people didn't believe it. Thankfully, Tim Weigel believed it [Weigel was a talented sportscaster at ABC-7 in Chicago]. He validated it by saying I broke the story Michael Jordan is going to play baseball."

But this story gets even juicer.

"The source who told me the story called me and said he didn't like the way I was treated. I'm going to tell you more. He's working out at IIT [Illinois Institute of Technology], and he's working out with a few players. So that's how I got the second part of the story, and then the entire media descended on IIT."

Raye-Stout's reward was to go to Sarasota, Florida, where the White Sox held spring training. And since she knew Michael was an early riser, Raye-Stout was the only one to get to training camp before the rest of the media.

Now, before you think, in the famous words of Paul Harvey, that that was the rest of the story, it was just the first half. There was Jordan's return to the Bulls!

"Remember, at that time the Bulls weren't champions anymore [Houston had won back-to-back titles in 1994 and 1995]. So some of the media stopped covering the Bulls. I was at the Berto Center, where the Bulls held their practice sessions. I was doing some free-lance work for a Florida radio station, and my friend says Michael has walked out of spring training. The curtain was down, which was normal when the Bulls were practicing. You couldn't see practice, but you could hear it. And I'm listening, and I say to myself, *That's not a normal practice*. I knew what a practice sounded like when Michael was there. When this person called telling me Michael had quit playing baseball, I got another call from a friend of a player saying Michael was there. So it wasn't hard for me to put two and two together. I kept quiet and didn't tell anyone in the media room what was going on."

Now it was time for the media to be allowed onto to the practice floor and talk to head coach Phil Jackson.

"I waited until everyone left, and as Phil was walking off the floor, I said, 'I hear Michael is here and working out.' And he said, 'Yeah, yeah, he is.' Then I walked back in to see if there were any players left, and I said, 'B.J. Armstrong, Michael is here with you guys?' He said, 'Yeah, yeah,' and nothing much more after that. And that was enough. I had a player and coach saying Michael is working out. So I called the station and said, 'Michael is back.' And that's how I got the story."

The respect for Raye-Stout had already been there, but it grew even greater with the breaking of both those stories. The object is to stick with it, have solid sources, and make sure you have all the facts. Cheryl Raye-Stout did, and she continues to work her sources. Who knows what big stories she'll break next?

# Kenny McReynolds

KENNY MCREYNOLDS has been one of Chicago's most influential and inspirational sportscasters for over 40 years. He's defied gangs, disappointment, over 40 surgeries, and a declaration of death! It's as if he's indestructible.

I've come to the conclusion, I think he is!

McReynolds has been a beacon in the African American community, where he's hailed as a true leader. But he's far more than that. McReynolds is omnipresent. Name a game or sporting event, and you're likely to see him there. His professionalism, intellect, easygoing nature, and infectious personality have made McReynolds one of our industry's favorite people to be around.

McReynolds was born in the Wentworth Gardens housing project, down the street from Comiskey Park, the home of the Chicago White Sox before it was replaced by the new park in 1991. It's why McReynolds is such a huge White Sox fan. Then the family moved to the Ida B. Wells project about a mile away. It was a dangerous area where he learned how to run and run fast, dodging bullets being fired by gang members. He was mostly spared by the gangs, who knew he was an athlete, and his stern mother, whom he was more afraid of than the gangs! McReynolds eventually managed to become part of the University of Chicago's track club, even though he wasn't a student there. He was fast—fast enough to be invited to the U.S. Olympic trial in 1976. He was only 14! But McReynolds played basketball, too, and hurt his knee. He had to have the first of those many surgeries but worked hard enough to regain his speed. He went down to St. Louis for the 1980 track and field trials and beat the likes of Ivory Crockett and Houston McTear, both of whom became international track stars. But because the U.S. boycotted the 1980 summer games in Moscow, McReynolds's dreams of competing in the Olympics were dashed.

It was the iconic and late Chet Coppock who got McReynolds started in the business, answering his call about wanting to see a roller derby match Coppock was broadcasting at the time. Coppock actually picked him up at his home and took him to the broadcast truck where he could hear how it all worked. It was after that that he declared he would go into communications. And his close relationship with Coppock was cemented. From there, McReynolds would eventually begin his Sunday morning sports show on WCIU TV: *Sports Edition*. He's done more than 1,000 shows, along with covering every sports team in town, but even more important, he established relationships with countless athletes, management personnel, politicians, and media members. And McReynolds is still part of the play-by-play team covering high school football and basketball, something he's done for more than 20 years. He was also an assistant basketball coach at DePaul, won local Emmy awards for his show, and was inducted into the Chicagoland Sports Hall of Fame in 2017.

*Ofman Appearing on* Sports Edition *with McReynolds*

I met Kenny in a press box, of course. The first thing I noticed is how dapper he dressed, and it hasn't changed. If he's not nattily outfitted in a classy suit or sport coat, you might see him in a track suit. Either way, he fit into a rather lively group of chatty radio and TV people who sat together and usually caused angry writers to chastise us for talking too much. Kenny can talk about anything, not just sports. His personality is so engaging, you can't help but like and respect him. He can tell stories with the best of them, and considering I've probably run into him a few thousand times, I've heard a few of them.

One of those stories has to do with his induction into the Chicagoland Hall of Fame in 2017, an event he couldn't attend because of a serious health issue. It's one of those stories you might find hard to believe.

"What happened was I had a tumor removed from my left shoulder. After the surgery, I told the doctors I didn't feel right and I shouldn't go home."

This is probably why McReynolds is still around. The doctors said he was okay and sent him home, anyway.

"Two days later, I'm throwing up blood and I had a high temperature."

So, of course, McReynolds found a way to make light of this despite a 104° fever.

"My boss at Channel 26, Fred Weintraub, called me, and I told him I was Michael Jackson and I was going on a victory tour!"

Apparently, Weintraub wasn't that amused.

"He called 911 and told them to break my door down. But what happened was, I lived in this building and my mom is on the second floor. She sees the fire department use an axe to break the door down. She says she has the key, only my burglar alarm is on."

If this sounds like it could be a pilot for a TV movie, keep reading.

"My mother doesn't know the code to the alarm, and the police say, 'We can't take him out of here unless someone gives us the code.' So my mom is calling me 'Kenny,' and I don't know I'm

Kenny! I keep telling her I'm Michael, so she says, 'Michael, baby, please tell me the code,' and I give her the right code."

Back to the hospital, where McReynolds remembers he couldn't breathe.

"Every time I sat down, I was drowning in my own mucous, so they had to hold me up. My nephew held me up for seven hours!"

Perhaps we need to take a commercial break here.

"Eight doctors came in to determine what to do. I'd already had a series of heart operations. They hook up my heart to a heart monitor, and one doctor is screaming, 'His heart rate is down to 30! Now it's down to 10. Make a decision!' So I tell my nephew Evan, 'I'm the only guy to die the same day I get inducted into the Chicagoland Sports Hall of Fame.'"

Now you're wondering if this is an episode of the *Twilight Zone*.

"I looked out the corner of my eye, and I see the security guard. 'Dude, what are you here for?' He wouldn't say anything, so I say, 'Yo...why are you here?' He said, 'Do you really want to know?' He said, 'They wanted me to guard your body, because you're a celebrity—until your family comes to claim it.' When Bernie Mac died in the hospital, nurses were coming in taking pictures of him dead and selling them. I remember the doctor screaming at the other doctors, 'His heart is at 8!' The next thing I remember is opening my eyes and hearing a doctor say, 'Let's call it. The official date of death: October 2, 2017.' I said, 'That's a shame. Who died?'"

Skip any commercial breaks. This is too good to be true.

"My nephew yelled to the doctors, 'Look, he's talking.' What happened is, doctors used a defibrillator three times, and when you don't respond after the third time, that's when they declare you dead."

Not so fast!

There were several seconds when McReynolds didn't respond, so the doctor turned his back and made his declaration. It was then McReynolds opened his eyes and began speaking. He was very much alive.

"I ended up in the hospital 17 days."

So who wound up representing McReynolds at the Hall of Fame inductions?

"When the doctors downgraded me to critical, they called my friend Andre Dawson." Dawson is the Hall of Fame outfielder who spent six seasons with the Cubs and became very good friends with McReynolds.

"The doctors said, 'Kenny's not going to make it,' so Andre was on his way. He was riding a bicycle in Miami, where he lives. He jumped on a plane in a T-shirt and shorts, flew to Chicago, and bought some clothes when he got there. He came to the hospital and asked my mother, could he accept my award, and she said sure. Andre gave a wonderful speech for me. That's a true friend."

And that's quite a story from quite a guy! McReynolds is still hanging in there, despite all of those surgeries and that harrowing story. He can laugh at it now but wasn't then. Meanwhile, McReynolds continues to do *Sports Edition*, show up for all sorts of games and events, and do his weekly assignment as part of the high school sports play-by-play team.

Lucky him. Lucky us!

# Ryan Baker

THINK ABOUT this for a minute: how many sportscasters have made a successful move to the news business? Brent Musburger tried from 1978 to 1980, working with Connie Chung at KNXT-TV in Los Angeles. Keith Olbermann actually left ESPN, where he had fashioned a spectacular career and wound up hosting *Countdown*, a very successful news commentary program on MSNBC. Bryant Gumbel switched from covering sports for NBC to anchoring the *Today* show in 1982, where he remained for 15 years before moving to CBS's morning show for two and a half years. But he also returned to sports, having hosted *Real Sports with Bryant Gumbel* on HBO since 1995. In Chicago, two sportscasters of recent vintage come to mind. Corey McPherrin was a TV sports anchor/reporter in several markets before moving to back to his hometown in 1991. Nearly 20 years later, he made the switch at WFLD-TV to an early morning program called *Good Day Chicago*. He's been doing it ever since.

Ryan Baker made the switch at WBBM-TV in 2019, where he won several awards anchoring and reporting sports in town since 2003. A native of Chicago like McPherrin, Baker also worked in several markets before coming back home.

Baker is a creative, upbeat guy whose sportscasts were dotted with metaphors. His ebullient style was a magnet for viewers. I met Ryan when he returned to Chicago in 2003, where he was recruited from Orlando following the stunning death of Darrian Chapman. Chapman, a very solid and competent pro, had worked at WMAQ-TV for about three years. He was an avid hockey player and was preparing to play when he collapsed and died of a heart attack. He was only 37. Channel 5 was thrust into the unenviable position of having to find his replacement as fast as possible. Ryan had already fashioned an outstanding career in Orlando, where, over the course of nine years, he was twice voted best sportscaster. He also worked in Champaign and San Diego. And being a native of the Chicago area, he appeared to be the right fit. It only took a few months before the station hired him.

Ryan was born in the south suburbs and attended the University of Illinois, where he was the basketball manager for the "Flyin' Illini," the Fighting Illini team that made the NCAA Final Four in 1989.

Ryan is proud of his association with the U of I. He remains very much involved with the university, so it makes sense we offer this story that occurred while he was a student in Champaign.

"I think it's appropriate I tell you this story. It was the spring of 1988, which would have been March Madness, which would have been my freshman year. You might recall when Kansas won the national championship in 2022, sitting courtside was Danny Manning. Danny and the Miracles. That great Kansas team that won the national championship in 1988. So let's rewind the tape to selection Sunday in 1988."

This is where the young, bold, and perhaps slightly misguided Baker decided to make a stand.

"Kansas was kind of struggling getting into the tournament. The bids come out, and the fellas at the dorm are doing their brackets, and it's crazy to think at this point it's over 30 years ago. Anyhow, Oklahoma was the big dog. They were the favorite, with our Stacey King, Mookie Blaylock, and the whole crew. And they had Harvey Grant, not Horace."

Harvey and Horace are twins, and Horace was the starting power forward on the Bulls' first championship threepeat.

"At that time, one of my roommates was Stephen Bardo who was the point guard for Illinois [and an outstanding college basketball analyst for the last 23 years]. There was a lot of back and forth on who was going to win, who's the favorite to win the national championship. So one of the guys on the floor said, 'I'm going with Kansas!' And I'm going, 'Are you crazy? Have you watched Kansas?

They suck right now. There's no way Kansas is winning the national championship. It's going to be Oklahoma.'"

Baker was rather emphatic about this, so much so he decided to make a bet. No money involved here, just naked pride!

"I said, 'There's no way. If Kansas wins the national championship, I'll run buck naked at high noon through the Quad [the center of the U of I campus].' And, he said, 'You got a bet!'"

Mind you, I went to Southern Illinois during the mid-1970s, when the rage was not only streaking but a Halloween tradition in which students stood atop buildings in the heart of town without a stitch of clothing!

"I'm not thinking much of it, but then the first round, second round, Sweet 16, Elite Eight, and the next thing you know after spring break we come back, Kansas is in the Final Four! And everyone is looking at me and...okay, Baker, are you sweating a little bit? You didn't think they'd get past the first round. And here they are, Danny and the Miracles. His mystique keeps growing, and he's leading the Jayhawks to the Final Four."

Baker appears nonchalant. If he's sweating, it's not showing, but...

"It's semifinal Saturday. They win, and they're going to the national title game against Oklahoma, and I'm like, *Are you kidding me?*"

A lot of us either go out for the championship game or to a friend's house, and we might be thinking, *What are we going to wear?* In Baker's case, he's thinking about what he might not be wearing.

"You know how the story ends. Of course, Kansas wins the national championship for Larry Brown. So I said, 'Listen, I'm a man of my word.' As soon as the final horn sounds, they said, 'You don't have to go back to the Quad. Matter of fact, you don't have to do it.' It's a gentleman's bet, but I said, 'No, no, no, I'm not a welcher.' My old dormmates and Illinois alums will often remind me, that Ryan Baker stripped down to his skivvies and a pair of Air Jordans and a down coat. And I said, 'No, I'm going all the way.'... I did about a 100-yard dash from our dorm, which was Hopkins Hall, to the Illini Orange and back."

I decided not to consider any visual version of this event because, let's face it, Baker is in his mid fifties now, so I'm not sure how he looked back then. But I digress.

"And all I remember is everyone's face plastered against the window and like, 'This guy's crazy.' To this day Stephen [Bardo] said, 'I've learned a couple of things. One, you are crazy, and two, you are a man of your word.' Let's just say this was before social media. It turned into a Kardashian moment!"

Oh, to be young and stupid again!

Baker has moved forward. Not only has his professional life thrived, He's the father of two girls he's incredibly proud of.

Nice to know some good guys can win on every level.

Just keep your pants on, Ryan.

# Mike North

THERE IS no one word to that best describes Mike North, so here are a few: outrageous, gregarious, controversial, galvanizing, loyal, polarizing, unafraid, popular. Anyone who knows or has listened to North over the years might come up with other words, some of which we would consider less than desirable. One thing is for certain: North went from owning a hot dog stand to becoming the most talked about sports talker in Chicago!

When The Score (WSCR) first came on the air in January 1992, management took a gamble. It decided to hire this high school drop-out who was actually serving them some of those hot dogs from a stand called BeBe's. That's the first name of his longtime wife and partner. He convinced them to take their 820 signal on the AM dial (The Score moved to 1160 AM in 1997 and finally to 670 in 2000) and turn it into an all-sports station. North had leased time on one of their other stations and aired an NFL handicap show. But eventually management went along with North's idea and established Chicago's first all-sports radio station. North was teamed up with former Chicago Bears offensive lineman and Harvard-educated Dan Jiggetts. It seemed like an unlikely pairing but quickly became a rousing hit. North dubbed himself the everyman host, and his popularity grew, although so did the animosity brought about by some of his comments. He was the station's sharp-tongued, leading personality who helped grow the ratings and its sponsorship. This is where the word *galvanizing* fits. Some sponsors loved him and were happy to spend money to hear him vent. The station and eventual parent company CBS also loved him enough to pay him very handsomely. At one point North was earning $1.5 million annually.

North would eventually leave the station in 2008 to join a company led by David Hernandez. They worked on an Internet project called Chicago Sports Webio. It debuted in April 2009, before anyone realized that Hernandez was running a Ponzi scheme to fund this and another project. Nine weeks later, Webio was history, as was Hernandez, who got sentenced to 16 years in jail. Some employees who were part of Hernandez's other business venture, Nex Step Medical, were out thousands of dollars. Some of us who were part of the Webio operation scrambled to find new jobs. North would eventually land with Fox Sports and today has his own show on YouTube titled *The Mike North Advantage*. He also shares a weekly gambling show with Carmen DeFalco on WMVP-ESPN 1000.

North is a guy from the Chicago neighborhoods. He was born in Edgewater, dropped out of Senn High School, and worked for the city. He once told me he picked up garbage after the Pope held mass in Grant Park, and 10 years later he was broadcasting the Bulls' first title celebration from that same park.

North was born to talk and raise hell on the radio. He called a Cubs Korean-born pitcher a "Chinaman," eviscerated former White Sox manager Al López, and pretty much took on all comers. This is where the word *unafraid* comes in. Rarely, if ever, did North back down from a verbal fight. It's what endeared him to his growing legion of fans.

I didn't know "Pappy" (his longtime nickname) until the station's introduction to the media in late December 1991. Little did I know this veteran radio sports journalist was about to come face to face with this enormous type A personality. I almost immediately hit the road for spring training in Mesa (with the Cubs) and Sarasota (with the White Sox). My job was not only to report but to procure guests for his show and others, and Pappy was pretty demanding. Just ask Jesse Rogers, his longtime producer and current baseball reporter for ESPN. But it wasn't until I started anchoring the sports weekdays did I get my real taste of Pappy. His acidic tongue reached out like an octopus's tentacles. He spared no one, including yours truly, but here's another word I used to describe him earlier: *gregarious*. North could put his arm around me, tell me I'm great while making me laugh uproariously. It wasn't like he was some split personality;

Pappy was complicated and you just had to learn how to deal with him. He could heap praise or criticize, but he always had my back. When Webio folded, he called several of us to his home and gave us each a check for $2,000.

Pappy also threw some wild parties at his old Park Ridge home, which he called, appropriately enough, "Pappy Land." Back then he could drink like no one I'd seen before. He would also visit familiar haunts in town on what was known as "the World Tour." It seemed like everyone knew him and enjoyed his company. But then Pappy went cold turkey and has been sober now for more than 16 years.

North was a great two-part interview. I expected nothing less. He traced the evolution of The Score to the man who decided to heed his advice.

"Danny Lee, in my opinion, was one of the greatest radio men who ever lived. [Lee passed away in December 2020.] He owned WXRT, an alternative rock station in Chicago. They used to come into my hot dog stand—Lin Brehmer, Norm Winer, Terri Hemmert. These radio personalities used to bring rock stars to the hot dog stand: Robert Plant, Johnny Hiatt, people like that."

North was starting to get noticed for his NFL handicap show, which he brokered through Lee in 1989. He heard Lee was about to start a jazz or country station on the 820 frequency. That's when he went into action.

"One day he comes into the hot dog stand, and I say, 'Why are you going to start a jazz station? Why don't you start a sports station?' And he looks at me says, 'Why would I do that?' And I say, 'Because there are some dozen cities already with all-sports stations.' He answered, 'Ah,' and walked out with his food."

North was not deterred. He chased Lee to his car in a driving rain despite a long line in the restaurant. "He's got his window down, and Seth Mason, his partner, was sitting shotgun. [Mason passed away in July 2020.]" North was yelling at the two. "Start a sports station!" he demanded. "They roll the window up on me and drive off."

But Lee had a revelation when he bought the Sunday *Tribune* and *Sun-Times*.

"He went to the entertainment section and saw some three to four prevalent ads. But when he went to the sports section, he counted some 27 to 30 ads, mostly aimed at men."

That Monday morning, they met in the conference room at WXRT. The staff wondered what he was going to do, a jazz or cool country station on 820.

"He said, 'We're going to start a sports station.' The staff went nuts and said, 'You're going to listen to the goofy hot dog guy?'"

He did and the rest is history. I was also an original member of The Score, and it didn't take long for the staff at WXRT become very friendly and engaging. We were crammed into this tiny building just big enough to house WXRT. Now it had two stations and one was very testosterone driven.

North has come a long way from picking up garbage in the park.

"One day, I came home and said to Be, 'I really screwed myself, I'm not going to be anything.' It's 1982 and I'm picking paper and raking leaves in Grant Park."

BeBe was the voice of reason.

"She said, 'Why don't we open a hot dog stand? We can do this.'"

And they did. Only they opened more than one.

"We bought the first place for five grand in bankruptcy and sold it two years later for 40 grand. That was big money back then. Then we opened BeBe's, and people were coming from all over...police department, Schurz High School, WXRT. I used to mop the floor at night and listen to Chet Coppock. [Coppock was a sportscaster in Chicago for more than 40 years.] I said, 'You know what? I want to get into sports radio.' And BeBe said, 'How are you going to do that?'"

That's when North brokered time at WSBC (AM 1240), another radio station owned by Danny Lee. He paid Lee $200 an hour for the privilege.

Fast forward to 2004. North already was being paid $150,000 annually by The Score. His contract was coming up. Rather than deal with CBS officials in Chicago, North did an end-around and met with then CBS honcho Dan Mason in Washington, D.C.

"They just lost Howard Stern and Jonathon Brandmeier. I made the calculated decision, Will they lose me? I don't think they want to. Dan Mason said, 'What do you want,' and we cut the deal in four hours."

That's how the shrewd North fashioned an unprecedented five-year deal worth $7.5 million. "I outsmarted the smart guys. I asked some agents, 'How much do you think I could make?' And they said a million. Some of them are still active, and they're dumber than a box of rocks!"

But in 2008 North was offered a new deal worth half of what he was making. "I turned it down, and some people said, 'You're out of your mind!' I said, 'If I take that pay cut, it will affect everybody else.'"

Then came Chicago Sports Webio.

I was there when a nervous and sweaty David Hernandez, dressed in a three-piece suit, called a staff meeting at Webio's home office in suburban Morton Grove. He accused North of questioning his business irregularities, which was why he fired him, his wife BeBe, and associate Jeff Schwartz. But one of the producers, reading from his cellphone, told Hernandez he was under federal investigation. Hernandez claimed this was untrue and declared he was going to lunch and would be back in a half hour. He never returned and was subsequently arrested a week later in downstate Normal, Illinois.

Working with North for 17 years was quite an experience. I've never met anyone like him and I doubt I ever will. Mike turned 70 in 2022, but his show on YouTube is still going strong. And he's built a following with Carmen DeFalco on their weekly gambling show on ESPN 1000 called *The Odds Couple*.

I always marveled at North's uncanny ability to drink, then come to work the next day as if he hadn't had a sip the night before. I kind of felt like he was indestructible. Funny thing: I still do.

# Dan Bernstein

ONE THING you can never say about Dan Bernstein is that he's boring. Whether he's talking about a Bears trade, fishing, food, music, or movies, Bernstein can carry his weight with just about anyone. From this fresh-faced Duke grad, who joined 670 The Score in 1995 to a more mellow version from the one you heard clearing the deck with longtime partner Terry Boers, "Bernsy," as he's best known, has run the gamut. He's managed to work with myriad cohosts without perceptibly missing a beat. He's called play-by-play of DePaul basketball and covered the Bears as a reporter. But, over time, he's established himself as the face of the station, a designation once owned by Mike North, an original member of the station.

When I mentioned "clearing the deck" in regard to Bernstein and cohost Terry Boers, I was referring to how this pair generated a huge following by tackling all topics and many times taking no prisoners, especially with callers to the show. The vitriol especially emanated from Bernstein, who had little patience and suffered no fools. But the two worked so well together because of their integrity and sense of humor. Boers, whom I consider the best sports talker in the city's history, was exceptionally quick-witted but needed some time to mesh with Bernstein. The duo eventually clicked, and their show lasted a Chicago sports radio record 17 years.

And when it comes to food, consider brain food, as in Bernstein being erudite. His vocabulary can be challenging at times and his highbrow approach a bit overwhelming. But the message and creativity have been well-received by his very loyal audience.

More important, perhaps, is Bernstein's tremendous devotion to the Children's Oncology Services. He is a member of the board of directors and emcees the annual charity poker event, Camp One

Step. It provides free year-round experiences for children with cancer. The 2023 event raised more than $150,000!

I first remember meeting Bernsy during a station function at some bar. He was absolutely thrilled to join our rather disjointed and sometimes pugnacious family. It didn't take him long to fit in and gain a following during his stint as solo host and Bears reporter. He added a unique flavor I enjoyed, although at times I would consider it a bit sour for my personal taste. It was his arrogance that rubbed me the wrong way. But I managed to understand it was an unintentional arrogance, and over time I came to realize what a valuable human being Bernsy is both to the station and the community.

Bernsy, like pretty much all of us, was weaned on sports, but it's interesting to note just what eventually drew him to the media business.

"Probably laziness," he admitted.

This prompted my response: "*Laziness?*"

"Because the idea of not wanting to go to law school because I never had a passion for it," he explained. "I majored in English, but there were a lot of factors, and I think one of the factors was that in high school I competed in a pretty high level in acting and speaking. It was called, Humorous Interpretation Dramatic Duet Acting, Humorous Duet Acting, and something called Impromptu Speaking. This happened all through IHSA forensics.

"In college, for the English majors, the Duke drama department was almost like a code share with the English department, where drama courses could count toward your English major, and that opened a whole world of cool stuff!"

They let Bernstein craft his concentration within his major.

"I ended up concentrating in American comedy and humor, and I had no idea this is what you study in college primarily. It made it like it wasn't work. And then concurrently, the student television station there, Cable 13 with no faculty involvement, was only student run."

Bernstein recalled how the place was dingy and run-down with mediocre equipment and few motivated people.

"But we got lucky with a group of people in the sports department who all arrived at the same time and looked around and said, 'Is nobody doing this? We can just do shows?' So, over time, we got a really motivated group of people who said, 'Wait a second, we could do play-by-play for basketball and football games?' Sure! All we need is someone to work the camera and someone to wire up this old truck that doesn't work anymore. And we did!"

For Bernstein, the experience of being able to do play-by-play really got him going.

"That got me press passes, and that got me into the heyday, the absolute heyday of ACC basketball. There's Jim Valvano, and there's Dean Smith, and there's Bobby Cremins and a young and not-so-famous Mike Krzyzewski. Duke wasn't Duke then. So four Final Fours and a senior year national championship later, and a multimillion-dollar investment by the school in the student station later, all of a sudden I thought, *This is something I can do.*"

Years later, Bernstein was thrust into the role of being Terry Boers' partner, this after the station decided to change the original partnerships, meaning Boers' seven-year run with Dan McNeil was over.

"When it happened, a lot of partnerships were blown up, and there was a lot of ill-will and resentment because a lot of people thought this was Mike North's doing. So it took a while for the some of the resentment to simmer down. And you always had a lump in your stomach, because every day [Boers was] like, 'I'm retiring, I got to get out of this business.' It was hard for me. I'm 30 years old. I felt like a vet since I was doing this for five years, but your name is on a show and you're looking at the next part of your life and thinking, *Now what's going to happen if he walks away?*"

Again, Bernstein mocks Boers: "'I'm going back to the *Sun-Times*. I don't like it, I don't feel like it.' He could be cranky and moody but, when the light went on, it never mattered. He could be bitching about everything. He could be in terrible pain, he could have a stomach virus, but the moment that red light went on, he was Terry—quick and funny and ready to go for four hours.

"There were times where Boers would drift off into some unconscious train of thought and make me laugh so hard I had trouble breathing. Tears were rolling down my cheeks. And this could go on for a good five, 10 minutes!"

Originally, then program director Ron Gleason wanted to title the show *Boers and Bernsy*, but Bernstein protested. He said it was infantilizing. Bernstein also felt it was hiding him as a Jew. Boers fought for him, and eventually the show was titled *Boers and Bernstein*.

"That made a huge difference. Once I had that sort of vote, Boers could not have been more supportive. Then when the objective metrics start to tell you things are going well, then people stay out of your way."

This didn't stop Bernstein form disparaging one of the station's staple segments, "Who You Crappin'?"

"It sucked," Bernstein said. "The truth about it was it was mostly awful. Everybody loved the idea of, 'Who You Crappin'?' It was great early because you could save things that happened on a Saturday that you read in the paper or heard. But that's what eventually happened. It was old news."

Suffice it to say, the show was a huge hit, and since Boers' retirement, Bernstein has gone through several cohosts, from Jason Goff to Connor McKnight to Leila Rahimi to his present-day partner, Laurence Holmes. Rahimi appears every Wednesday.

Bernstein likes what he calls "a steady job" and a well-paying one, at that. He would like to do more play-by-play, and who knows, that just might happen. But for now, Bernstein's "steady job" is a steady listen for many who have followed him now for over 25 years.

# Dan McNeil

DAN MCNEIL never met a comment he wouldn't make, and it got him in enough hot water, the burn marks are still there. One of Chicago's most popular and controversial sports talk show hosts, McNeil was an original at WSCR The Score and also spent considerable time working at WMVP-ESPN 1000. But his constant clashes with cohosts and management, plus an incendiary tweet about an ESPN-TV reporter in 2020 very likely ended his run on Chicago radio. McNeil was called a titan by Barrett Sports Media. Greg Solk, now the vice president of programming and operations for the Audacy stations in Chicago called McNeil, "Every man's man." Listeners enjoyed McNeil's candid, if sometimes reckless comments refreshing. They also admired his honesty when discussing his personal life, whether it was about one of his children, who is autistic, to grappling with depression and addiction.

He had a very successful run with Terry Boers when The Score debuted in 1992. But seven years later, the station broke up the duo and paired McNeil with Dan Jiggetts, who had been working with another iconic figure at the station, Mike North. McNeil didn't want to work with Jiggetts and suffered through two years before teaming up with Harry Teinowitz and John Jurkovic on rival WMVP. Mac, Jurko, and Harry became *The Afternoon Saloon*. It was a huge hit but also involved a major clash between McNeil and Teinowitz. It also involved a 2007 suspension when McNeil made a crude remark about longtime Chicago publicist Lissa Druss. In early January 2009, McNeil and his $600,000 salary were let go. He wound up back on The Score and spent five more years there, working with Matt Spiegel. He had a third stint on the station with Danny Parkins before an ill-conceived tweet concerning ESPN's Maria Taylor's outfit got him fired. He tweeted about Taylor: "NFL sideline reporter or host for the AVN annual awards presentation?" It refers to the annual pornography awards show presented by *Adult Video News.*

McNeil would eventually launch a weekly show on WJOB in Hammond, Indiana, and now has a podcast with Bet Rivers Casino.

I first encountered Dan in the mid 1980s when he was a producer for Chet Coppock's *Coppock on Sports* nightly gabfest on WMAQ radio. Dan was a go-getter nicknamed "Dangerous Dan." That nickname was a harbinger of things to come. He often clashed with Coppock but also said there was no one who advanced his career more. I appeared on the show as a regular contributor, so I dealt with Dan and enjoyed the fact that he was a big hockey fan like myself. Eventually, we would cross paths again as original members of The Score in January 1992. He worked alongside Terry Boers, and as the sports anchor I interacted with them during their show. It was during one encounter when I was covering a game at Wrigley Field, and I declared that a Sammy Sosa homer was "a towering line drive." This elicited an immediate response from Dan, who challenged me on the term. It became one of the hallmark moments on the radio station, and I still get people on social media referring to "a towering line drive."

I've always found Dan to be a complicated yet caring person. He clearly wears his emotions on his sleeve, something that has also cost him professionally. When we conducted what turned into a two-part episode, Dan didn't blanch. He was open and honest about personal issues.

"I was a suicide survivor. When I was 18 my mother took her own life. I knew I was different in fifth grade. I woke up one morning, I remember it so vividly. It was the first nice day of the spring and I felt paralyzed, and I didn't want to go to school. I told my parents, 'I'm not going to school,' yet I couldn't define what was ailing me. What I wanted was my door locked, my 45 collections, my baseball cards, and total isolation."

McNeil believed this wasn't right, because physically he felt fine.

"That's brain chemistry," McNeil continued. "Fortunately, people have become smarter to what mental illness is."

This is when McNeil slowly began to realize he had issues that would haunt him in his adult life. "Fortunately, I started treating this brain-chemical deficiency about 20 years ago. But I inherited this from my mother, along with my predisposed condition to be an addict."

McNeil was almost dispassionate in describing his ordeals. "I've loved weed since I was a teenager, but unfortunately that graduated to a lot more dangerous substances." McNeil admitted to having an unhealthy relationship with cocaine in the late 1990s, as he tried to numb the pain of his middle son's autism. But McNeil was also dealing with having to do a show with Dan Jiggetts, with whom he didn't get along. "I would do a show that made me sad and I would wind up in a saloon in Hammond until 4:00 AM snorting blow!"

Then McNeil dabbled in pain meds after having his spine fused in 2007. "After the fusion, I discovered the 10-milligram Norco—the little yellow bird, I would call them. That was something different than I had ever experienced before. That was a high that drew mean. 'As needed' on the bottle didn't apply to me."

McNeil's drug addiction was in full force. He wrestled with that as his primary addiction for the next six to seven years. "A bottom is a bottom, and mine is to be alone. My bottom is not to be in touch with anyone other than my kids and my wife, to go away and hide and not give back."

This was a stunning admission by McNeil, who grappled with this issue until he finally sought help. "What truly makes me happy is being part of the fraternity and a community, whether it's with my high school pals, my radio fraternity, my fantasy football league, or my audience. I like that, I thrive on that! But when I was in the throes of that opioid addiction, I wanted nothing to do with that. I was rejecting what made me happy."

Fortunately for McNeil, he never flirted with thoughts of suicide. The reason for that is pretty simple: it's his nearly 30-year-old autistic son, Patrick. McNeil said he would never do to his son what his mother did to him. He calls Patrick his best friend.

Today, McNeil is in a better place.

"I'm happy today more than I'm sad. I've treated my depression with chemicals and talk therapy. I don't do opioids and haven't danced with the devil known as cocaine in many, many years. So I will smoke my weed and have a Diet Pepsi and be grateful for every day I have."

What was so riveting about this interview was McNeil's continued candor. He returned to his mother: "When your mom isn't available, as my mom was not throughout my life—I was five when she was first institutionalized—what came with her suicide, and I didn't know it consciously for a good 20 years, was she helped [me] not trust the female gender."

McNeil was far more reflective than he was emotional about this subject.

"I thought women would ultimately leave me. My mom wasn't available, my older sister wasn't available, she was a troubled kid. I started to think I have nothing to offer females. I was a guy's guy. I wish I sought therapy at the time more than I did."

McNeil eventually married and had three sons before getting a divorce and remarrying. One of those sons, of course, is Patrick.

"I think the worst day I had as the parent of an autistic boy was probably when he was four years old. It was early in the evening, and his older brother Van was doing homework at the kitchen table. Patrick tried to convey to me what he wanted from the freezer."

Verbal skills were much tougher for Patrick then, but he became much better as he aged.

"Speech was very difficult, and he was trying to get something from the freezer. He obviously didn't get what he wanted, so he started to bang his head on a hard ceramic tile floor. I looked at his brother, who slumped in his chair and started to sob, and I tried to comfort this hysterical four-year-old boy who couldn't make speech. I never felt the helplessness that completely bankrupts my soul."

But Patrick is much happier today. He's made marked progress, and though he'll never be able to live on his own, he's a very happy young man.

McNeil has had one hell of a life, admitting he's made a lot of his own messes. "It's been a challenge, but I blame myself."

McNeil doesn't envision getting back into full-time radio, nor does it appear either of the Chicago all sports stations are prepared to hire him again. "I don't need that. I did it for a long time. I feel pretty good now."

# Jonathan Hood

JONATHAN HOOD, aka J. Hood, is the cohost along with David Kaplan of a morning sports talk show on WMVP–ESPN 1000 in Chicago. The show is in its third year, but Hood is nearing his 30th in the business. A jack-of-all-trades but as funny a guy as there is in the business, Hood has carved out a successful career through tremendous determination and talent. He's a play-by-play announcer (UIC Flames baseball and basketball), a podcaster (*Under the Hood* and *Good Karma Wrestling*) and even an instructor (Illinois Media School).

Hood grew up a TV rat. He was glued to the TV, but not just watching weekly shows. He would also watch the news and was an avid listener of the radio. It's the reason he's in the business today.

Hood began his career at WSCR The Score, Chicago's first all-sports radio station, where he was a producer and then an on-air talent. He moved on to ESPN 1000, though there was a sort of day trip to the ill-fated Chicago Sports Webio, an Internet radio project that folded after nine weeks because it was operated by someone running a Ponzi scheme. But Hood would resurface at ESPN 1000, where he's been a fixture ever since.

I met J at The Score, where he joined a group of young and enterprising producers who would go on to have very successful careers. It was easy to see why J succeeded. He managed to use his wit and devilish sense of humor to break through on one particular show, but also demonstrated a solid knowledge of the sports landscape and translated that into his own show. I would appear on J's show from time to time, but the time I remember the most was the Cubs postgame celebration in Atlanta, when in 2003, they won their first playoff series since winning the World Series in 1908! I was on the air live from the clubhouse using my cellphone to relay interviews back to J and our listeners. This took place for a good 20 minutes. It was one of the great highlights of my career, and I was glad to share it with J.

One of J's career highlights was doing a national show on ESPN radio with his dear, late friend Jeff Dickerson. They came from different backgrounds, yet their bond was extremely tight. Dickerson died in late December 2021 from cancer, two and a half years after his wife also died from the dreaded disease. JD was one of the most respected and beloved figures in our industry. J could make Dickerson laugh so hard, it was worth listening to the show just for that.

"The whole overarching point about this business is to have fun with it," Hood said. "Yes, it's great to be paid and to figure out what's next, but while you're in it you're supposed to have fun. And with Jeff, we had a lot of fun together. While working at ESPN 1000, an opportunity came up for me to do a national show. The whole point of me coming to ESPN 1000 in August of 2005 was eventually to go national."

Hood liked the perspective of talking to a national audience about everything, so he relished the opportunity to fulfill the challenge. So, after finding out that JD needed a partner for a new show they were going do on Saturday nights, he was chosen because he had already done shows on ESPN 1000.

"I get an opportunity to work with JD, and right before the show I'm nervous. I'd already been in the business a long time, and when you take the microphone you have a little bit of tension, but not condors in your stomach! I'm thinking, *Oh, my God. I'm with JD, but it's national.* And I'm pacing the hallways, something I don't normally do."

One of Hood's producers, Eric Ostrowski, did his best to calm his nerves. At that point Hood calmed down and reminded himself he was working with his friend, and from there he and JD did five solid years of weekends together.

But there was one particular Sunday in late January 2020 when they were preparing to do a show, and something occurred that was life-changing, to say the least.

"We were working a 3:00 to 7:00 shift, and we were going through our notes. Cowboys here and LeBron there, and we'll find out some stuff here. We'll talk about baseball and have the late Pedro Gomez, who was a weekly guest and a great guest. So it's about four minutes before we go on the air, and the producer at Bristol, Connecticut, says, 'Hey, guys, we're getting news...something's going on with Kobe Bryant.' And we're thinking, *What's going on with Kobe?* He's retired and with his daughter, Gigi. Three minutes left.

"Producer—'Guys, we hear there's a helicopter, there's the helicopter went down. Stand by, we're getting more information.'"

At this point Hood is trying to make sense of this. Kobe's in a helicopter, and he and JD are wondering what the news is.

"Producer—'Two minutes, guys, the helicopter went down. Kobe and his whole family were in the helicopter, and it went down. There are casualties. Stand by.'

"So now we're panicking and going online to see if there's any information."

"Producer—'Guys, one minute, 60 seconds. Kobe's 'copter went down, and we believe his family was in it and maybe some of the Laker players.'"

Now, Hood and JD are wondering what to lead with. Is it still the Cowboys? Is it still LeBron?

"Producer—'Guys, 10 seconds. We just got word, Kobe and his family died in the helicopter. Five, four, three, two, go!'"

Welcome to the world of breaking news.

"JD and I are looking at each other, and JD is solid as a rock. He takes the information, takes a deep breath, and says, 'Ladies and gentlemen, welcome to ESPN radio. I'm Jeff Dickerson of Dickerson and Hood, and we just found out word from ESPN, Kobe Bryant has passed away.' And I'm a mess! I'm a mess, and he throws it to me, and I don't know what I said, but it probably wasn't English. I don't know what I said, but this is coast to coast national radio on an afternoon in which we thought we were going to be talking about the Cowboys or some other nonsense, and we find out an icon has just died."

During that period of time, the story was very sketchy. But this happens from time to time when there's a breaking story. No one was quite sure the extent of what had transpired and who exactly was involved.

"The idea you have a minute to go before showtime, and the producer says no matter what you gotta go, because Kobe's died. *Go!* The thing that will always resonate with me is JD was a rock. He was steady, given that news. I don't know what I said, but I just have to give my partner so much credit because that was a daunting task to get on the microphone and start having memories of Kobe Bryant, and he just died within seconds of going on the air. We did that show for four hours.

That was quite a memorable show for Hood, who wanted to make sure he related just how strong JD was: "Strong enough to support his wife through her cancer and strong and defiant through his. He said in hospice to me, 'These doctors don't know me. If I can just get to Christmas, I think I'll be okay.'"

JD got to Christmas but three days later lost his battle with cancer. He was 43.

This story was so important to tell because it describes the type of friendship we all hope to have. I did with someone I met in high school. We were very close and loved to spend time together and with others. But 10 years ago, my dear friend Ronney Strohl died from ALS and dementia. I think of him all the time the way Jonathan Hood must think of Jeff Dickerson, with great joy.

# Marc Silverman

IF YOU say the name "Silvy" in Chicago, you're likely referring to Marc Silverman, longtime sports radio host at WMVP-ESPN 1000, who partners with Tom Waddle in the afternoons. Their partnership of 17 years is one of the longest in Chicago sports radio history. Silvy, who attended Southern Illinois University as I did, began his Chicago career as an intern at WGN radio in 1995, and thanks to some guile, took advantage of a situation. The station had no one covering nighttime sports. He took on the task of covering Bulls and Blackhawks games. Well, as luck would have it, there was a rumor Michael Jordan was ending his baseball career and wanted to return to the Bulls. The rumor got even hotter as Jordan was expected at the Berto Center, the Bulls' practice site in suburban Deerfield. The media descended, including a young Silvy, who called himself a lowly intern. While Jordan didn't show, Silvy interviewed a number of players and head coach Phil Jackson. He went back to the studio and produced a "Mission Impossible" piece (named after the popular 1960s show). His piece was played on the air, and the next day Silvy went back to the Berto Center, where this time Jordan showed up. He got his interview, and lo and behold, a few days later WGN hired him as a part-timer. A year later, it became full-time. This is what you call "right time, right place."

Silvy is a native of Chicago, and like many of us in the business, always wanted to be in the sports media. He grew up listening to the late Chet Coppock on AM 1000 and WSCR The Score. I worked there, and Silvy was gracious with his praise about me. Although we both attended Southern Illinois University, we were a number of years apart. Silvy tried out for the sports department at SIU, but his sound didn't impress the student sports director, so he didn't make the cut. He was allowed to cover games and, in his second semester, made the staff. Silvy was a dean's-list student and eventually embarked on a career that took him to a small town in Iowa. Twenty-eight years later, he's become a prominent voice on Chicago radio.

Silvy's very passionate and loves to share pretty much everything on the air, from his rants to his personal life. But in 2020 he shared something life-altering that stunned and also galvanized his listeners and others who'd never heard his show.

"This was something I wanted to share," he said. "I got an ultrasound on a lymph node in my neck. They did a biopsy, and it was there where the doctor examined these larger lymph nodes that were way bigger than they should be."

Tears started to run down Silvy's face. At this moment in his life, he feared he had cancer.

"And, sure enough, on that Sunday before the biopsy, which we needed to confirm, the CAT scan came back, and the doctor called me and said, 'All the signs of the scan confirm you have a form of lymphoma.'"

The idea Silvy decided to share this with his audience became therapeutic for him. The more he spoke about it, the more open he got.

"It was about a month from the diagnosis when I went public, because I wanted to make sure all the i's were dotted and the t's crossed. I knew what I had and the treatment would be so I can give all the information possible on the air."

What surprised Silvy the most was the reaction. It was much greater than he ever expected.

"I thought there would be concerned people. I thought I'd get some love, but never did I think I would get the outreach I got."

It was similar to what happened to Eddie Olczyk, the former analyst for the Chicago Blackhawks who revealed on the air he had stage 3 colon cancer. The outpouring of emotion and support was staggering. "Silvy Strong" became the rally cry, replete with T-shirts, whose sales would go to charity.

"Eddie went through this a year or two before me, but it was during the time he was going through this he was doing a lot of shows with David Kaplan on our radio station [Kaplan and Olczyk are very close friends]. I knew Eddie, but I never knew him well. But I got to know him more when he was doing all of these appearances, and I love the guy. My ears always perked up when he was candid, and it goes back to, *Did I have an obligation to tell people?* or *Did I want to share?* It stood out to me like, *Wow, listen to what Eddie's going through. Listen to how real he is."*

One of the first phone calls Silvy made was to Olczyk, even before his mother! He didn't want to scare her. He called Eddie because it stood out to him what he had to go through, what he had to deal with, how successful it turned out to be for him.

He told Olczyk, "This is what I'm dealing with, and I need to find out more.... Can you help me with this?... Can you tell me more about this? He was fantastic, and to this day, three years of remission, he'll still text me out of the blue, 'Thinking of you,' with a praying emoji and to let me know I popped up in his brain. He did that through my entire process of going through chemo."

Silvy quickly found out how people reacted to his situation.

"It's incredible, and what people told of this army of people are either survivors or going through it themselves. I can't tell you how many people who had it worse than me. One is no longer with us. He was a listener who passed away from brain cancer, and while he was going through his battle sent me a key on a necklace and the key said COURAGE. He was thinking of me, even though he was going through his own fight with cancer, and he had it much worse than I did. He was there for me, and there are a lot people like that, people who are selfless."

What that did for Silvy was lift him up. And to anyone with a cancer diagnosis who DMs him, he gives advice on how to deal with the mental aspect and roll with the punches. But make no mistake about it, this was a gut-punch to Silvy and his family. At that time, he had two very young boys. While sharing the news on the air was therapeutic, his original reaction was anything but.

"Oh, my! There was a day in that first week of April. I can still remember it. I was seeing my internist. I had the lymph node that was swollen in my neck, but I had one in my groin that worried me more. He told me the bloodwork worked out well, but he still wanted me to get a biopsy on it to rule out cancer. So I thought I was going to get it ruled out, but I had lymphoma. And I'll never forget coming home that night after going to work, and my wife had to hold me, hold me like a baby, and I just cried in her arms. All these dark thoughts go through your brain. My kids are five and three at the time, and, like, are they going to know me? Are they going to remember me? What if I'm gone? Is there someone who's going to replace me that they think of as their dad?"

All these thoughts, which Silvy described as selfish, permeated through his brain. I can tell you from my own, albeit different experience, those thoughts creep in.

"I'm thinking, *Am I going to die?* You deal with it for the 24 to 48 hours, and then what I've always done is, you get to work. Okay, now what? I start researching it, and that's where all the mental stuff came into play. I believe if the mind is not right, the body won't follow. So I wanted to heal the mind so the body could heal."

It's been more than three years since the diagnosis, but Silvy says he's doing fine now.

"I have energy. Cancer patients know it's a dark place, even after you're in remission. It's not a fault of everybody, but a lot of people think once you're in remission, everything is great. There's a lot of guilt, there's a lot of questions, there's a lot of worry. Then the body has to recover from chemo. To beat the cancer, the chemo really beats the hell out of your body. My workouts weren't going well, I was overly tired, I was overly crabby. Right now, I'm 99 percent feeling right. I'm 52 and getting old!"

Fifty-two and getting old? Really? I'll be 70 at the end of December, even though I look like I'm 69½!

"I'm not 35 anymore. I'm not 40. I used to be one of the young guys at the station. I'm chasing around two young kids, but yeah, I feel great. You get a lot of mixed emotions after what happened to JD."

JD was Jeff Dickerson, the football reporter for the station and a widely respected, admired, and cherished person who died of cancer at 43, just two and a half years after his wife also succumbed to the dreaded disease.

"There' a lot of guilt there. It's ongoing, and it's why I've taken up the fight for the V Foundation." (The foundation is named after Jim Valvano, the former North Carolina State head basketball coach who died of cancer in 1993.) "We just can't continue to have these things happen, and we have to continue to eventually find cures for all these horrible diseases."

Silvy and Waddle continue their afternoon show, and Silvy hasn't missed a beat. He remains passionate, effervescent, and sharing everything from sports to his personal life.

No reason to stop now.

# David Kaplan

HE'S "KAP" or "Kapman" or "Kappy." Almost no one calls him by his real name, but David Kaplan has been a marquee figure in Chicago sports journalism for nearly 40 years. He went from writing the *Windy City Roundball Review* newsletter, to coaching, to becoming one of the city's most prominent sports personalities. And he's a tireless promoter. Just go to social media, where his posts come fast and furious. He's relentless in his pursuit of publicity, and it's worked very much in his favor. Kaplan has worked in all aspects of the media—print journalism, radio, TV, and social media. To say he's everywhere would be an understatement. Kaplan was a basketball junkie growing up. He was and still is a very avid Cubs fan. Upon leaving college at Hamline University in St. Paul, Minnesota, Kaplan embarked on a coaching career. He was an assistant coach at Northern Illinois University from 1982 to 1986 and was also a scout for two NBA teams. He devised the *Windy City Roundball Review* as scouting reports to college coaches. It got the attention of the late Chet Coppock, a legendary Chicago sportscaster who also was a self-promoter. All of this eventually led to Kaplan doing some college basketball play-by-play and being hired by WMVP-ESPN 1000 in 1993. Kaplan eventually landed at WGN Radio, where he replaced Chuck Swirsky, also a guest on my podcast. Swirsky left for Detroit, but he would eventually return to Chicago, where he's currently the radio voice for the Chicago Bulls. Kaplan also became the TV host for *SportsTalk Live*, a panel discussion show on Comcast SportsNet, now known as NBC Sports Chicago. He hosted that show for a dozen years. He was also heavily involved in the pre- and postgame shows for Chicago Cubs telecasts but left the station at the end of 2022.

Kaplan currently does morning sports radio on ESPN 1000 with partner Jonathan Hood, also a guest on my podcast. Kaplan's wife, Mindy, is an executive with Lou Malnati's Pizzeria.

How did I first meet Kap? Let's put it this way: you couldn't avoid him. Like I mentioned earlier, Kap was everywhere, but mostly doing his radio and TV shows. A gregarious self-promoter, Kap has a Rolodex of names in and out of the business that might double as an encyclopedia. I've asked for a few cell numbers over the course of time, and it wouldn't take but a minute for Kap to come up with it. I was also Kap's guest from time to time on *SportsTalk Live*, and it was always a joy to be there. He is very comfortable commanding the show and involving his guests. It was a shame when the show was canceled.

Kap is tireless worker. There were times he would arise at 4:00 AM, do his radio show, then head to the TV studio to do Cubs pre- and postgame shows, and not be home until midnight or later. I once asked Kap when he sleeps, and to paraphrase, he said, "I'll sleep when I'm dead."

Kap also loves to use social media at all hours of the day and night, even when he's on vacation. It never stops. He's quite a character, and a very generous one, with his time and ability to lend a helping hand. Kap is also a great storyteller. His interview was so good, I made it a two-parter.

Kap loves breaking stories (that massive Rolodex really does come in handy). Well, here's one of his greatest scoops—which turned out not to be a scoop—and it involves a former Chicago Bulls Hall of Fame player.

"After I started my newsletter," Kap said, "I started to work for a guy in Detroit who owned a trading card company."

The owner was doing a rookie draft pick card set and asked Kaplan if he would write on the backs of the cards and predict who the first-round picks for 1989 would be. Kap accepted.

"So I go to Port Smith, Orlando, and Chicago. These are all sites of pre-draft camps. And I'm dealing with agents, because as soon as these kids' eligibility was done, we would sign them to contracts. I make amazing contacts with these agents. I go down to the NBA Draft in Indianapolis and I get a call from one of these agents whose players I represented. He said, 'How would you like an exclusive?'"

There was no way in the world Kap would turn down an exclusive, so he went down to draft night, where the agent was going to give him exclusive interviews with the first three picks. Kap was working freelance for the old SportsChannel in Chicago. They sent him a cameraman. They did the interviews, but the cameraman had to drive the tapes back to Chicago. Such was the technology of the day.

"We're on the elevator and a guy is staring at me. 'Are you Kap?' he said. He then said, 'I'm going to see a lot of you.' 'Who the hell are you?' [Kap replies]. The guy rattles off two names who are big-time basketball agents. He said, 'Our No. 1 draft choice just got traded to the Bulls! I'm driving to O'Hare, where I will meet him and then he has to go pass a physical.'"

Kap's interest has been piqued. Scottie Pippen is going to Seattle for Shawn Kemp and Ricky Pierce!

I happened to remember this because I was also covering the draft, and we had heard whispers that Pippen was going to get traded.

Kap said, "No way!" The agent declared, "God's honest truth, but don't quote me."

"So I call his bosses and ask, 'Is Scottie Pippen being traded to Seattle for Shawn Kemp?' One of the bosses confirmed it. I call in on WMVP and break the story. It goes everywhere, and Dan McNeil is barbecuing me on the Score.

"Now the day goes on, and nothing is getting confirmed. It's 5:00 o'clock, and McNeil is destroying me, and I'm saying my career is over! I'm getting calls from bosses, and they say nothing's happening. Now the draft has started, and one of the TV announcers says there's a report Chicago has acquired Seattle's pick and traded Scottie Pippen for Shawn Kemp, but nothing's happened."
The news only got worse for the beleaguered Kap. Bulls general

manager Jerry Krause met the media and was asked about the trade rumor. He says, "I don't know where David Kaplan came up with that. We never approached Seattle."

Kap got destroyed in the media for the next three days.

"I know I was right! So it finally dies out. I'm coaching an AAU team, and I get a call from one of my subscribers to the newsletter."

This guy was an assistant coach with the Portland Trailblazers but used to be with Seattle.

Kap exclaimed, "You were at Seattle? Did you make a trade for Scottie Pippen?" And the assistant says, "That's a sore subject, and I don't want to discuss it." A perturbed Kap said, "I'm not answering any more questions until you tell me the truth." He then admitted, "We're trading a guy who has a lot of off-the-court issues, and the trade was done, and Jerry Krause leaked it to some asshole in the Chicago area. When he reported it, our fan base started to cancel season tickets because they couldn't believe 'the Reign Man' [Kemp] wouldn't be there."

You can imagine how Kap reacted.

"I look at him and said, 'That's not how it went down.' He said, 'How the hell would you know?' And I said, 'Because I'm the asshole in the Chicago media who reported it!'"

But Kap gained some measure of satisfaction, despite getting barbecued by a fellow sports talk radio host.

"The guy says, 'Dude, if you don't report that story, the deal gets done! You went on KJR radio in Seattle and reported the story, and that's when fan base started freaking out and canceling season tickets. And our owner came into our conference room and said he would not sign off on the trade. Even Shawn Kemp chimed in on radio. The fans said they would burn down the Coliseum if the trade went through. Ownership did call me and said they were going to make the trade, but then reversed it.'"

This story is far from over.

"So now, one of my best friends, Rick Majerus, dies. I go to the funeral. There's George Karl, coach of Seattle Supersonics, and I've never met him before. I walk up to him and say, 'Hey, George, David

Kaplan, I was a real close friend of Rick's.' I said, 'Can I ask you a question? Did you make a trade for the Bulls' Scottie Pippen?' 'Yeah, I did, and that asshole Jerry Krause F'd me, and the trade blew up.' So I said, 'That's not how it went down.' And he said, 'How would you know?' 'Because I'm the guy in the Chicago media who broke it.'"

Well, then, I think we have a movie script here.

Karl angrily replied, "If I would have seen you the next day, I would literally have punched you in the face! You singlehandedly broke up that trade, and let me tell you something, I know you got it from Krause.' And I said, 'That's not true. I got it from Shawn Kemp's agents!' He said, 'Oh, my God, I never knew that.'"

So Dan McNeil, take that. It was true.

Vindication, of sorts. Pippen would help lead the Bulls to six NBA titles.

# Lou Canellis

HE'S INEXORABLY tied to the Chicago Bears and Michael Jordan. He's a sportscaster with solid credentials and a personality to match. He's an entrepreneur and deeply involved with a restaurant. He's handsome, debonair, and the father of a lovely daughter.

Seriously, what more does Lou Canellis need?

"I'm an Oak Lawn kid, southwest suburbs [of Chicago], who wakes up every morning living the dream."

See what I mean?

Lou Canellis is the stuff dreams are made of. A guy who has it all, but you'd never know it because he keeps reaching for new heights—witness Avli, a Greek restaurant with several locations in the Chicago area that Canellis has a piece of and which has been a spectacular success. But Canellis was successful long before that, fashioning an outstanding career in broadcasting when all he wanted was to be a baseball player. It really started when he was a young boy and wanted to work at SportsPhone. He was so little he had to stand on a stool to pry the phone loose from its cradle. When it fell into the garbage can, he picked it up and dialed the number so he could listen to people like, yes, yours truly.

I'm blushing, trust me.

Well, Canellis got his wish and worked there where many others who made it in this broadcasting business did. How about Jeff Joniak (voice of the Bears), Chris Madsen, (once the voice of the Anaheim Ducks), the late Dave Wills (the beloved voice of the Tampa Bay Rays), and the late Les Grobstein, one of Chicago's most unique characters in Chicago sports media. In New York, Gary Cohen, the longtime voice of the Mets and Mike Walczewski (better known as "King Wally"), who is the public address announcer for the New York Knicks also started at SportsPhone! Quite a fraternity. From there, Canellis's career mushroomed. He became a sideline reporter during the Bulls championship runs, instantly turning himself into a household name. Part of that included the relationship he developed with Michael Jordan. He also worked for ESPN, covered two Olympic Games, won a half-dozen Emmys, and has been FOX 32's lead sportscaster for well over a decade.

Who doesn't like Lou? He exudes a magnetic personality. It's almost like you want to be around him just because. When I met him early in his career, I would also run into him while he was sunning himself at Oak Street Beach and I was riding my bike up and down the lakefront. Talk about living the life! But I quickly learned this dashing individual was very serious about his profession and worked diligently and tirelessly on his craft. Good looks can only get you so far.

My relationship with Lou took an even deeper turn when I met my future wife, Elizabeth, at a wedding in Springfield, Massachusetts. When I returned from an unreal weekend, I sat next to Lou at Halas Hall, where the Bears trained. He looked at me and exclaimed, I was a million miles away. He sensed something right away. I had yet to tell someone that I thought I met the woman of my dreams. Here I was, just shy of 35, confiding in this guy who was in his mid-twenties. Lou had a way with the girls, and it just seemed so natural for me to tell him what had happened. I didn't tell another soul for three weeks! A trust factor and a friendship developed instantaneously.

Growing up, Lou had to trust in himself first and make decisions that didn't exactly fit with his father's wishes. "I played baseball in high school," he said. "I was a pretty good player, had some opportunities to play away at college, [but] Dad wouldn't let me go. He wouldn't let me take advantage of scholarship opportunities. I was the oldest of three Greek boys."

Canellis explained that his dad was a dictator. No democracy in that household. His dad said he worked his whole life to send his kids to college, and baseball scholarships didn't matter. It really hurt the young Canellis. "I really didn't get a taste of what I was missing until I spent the weekend at Eastern Illinois in Charleston and also the University of Illinois in Champaign. I realized I was missing partying, girls, good times, being away from my parents. I came back home, and remember, my dad was a dictator. I loved him to death. I had the utmost respect for him. He was built like Charles Atlas, working in a laundry for 60 years."

This is when things started to change.

"My dad said, 'How was the weekend?' and I pointed my finger at him and said, 'You have ruined my life!' I went up to my room and frankly thought he would come upstairs and I was going to get my rear end kicked."

But Canellis had another thing coming, which he didn't expect.

"Instead, he sat on the bed with me and asked me to explain why I had broken down and why I was so upset. I did and he recommended seeing if I could still play baseball away at those schools." It wasn't possible, however, as it had been two years since Canellis had played competitively. But he almost went to the University of Florida to enjoy college life.

"But at that point Brian Wheeler, who I worked with at WLUW at Loyola University and eventually became the voice of the Portland Trailblazers, and who was also the voice of Loyola basketball for 20 years—Lou Canellis's old roommate—suggested I send a tape to Fred Huebner at SportsPhone, and I got hired! This was two weeks before I was going to go to Florida! And Dad said, 'I'm going to let you make the decision, but if you choose to stay home I will help you get an apartment on the Gold Coast so you could walk to SportsPhone.'" SportsPhone was located on the 31st floor of the 100-story John Hancock building, and the Gold Coast was and still is one of the city's most fashionable neighborhoods.

"I stayed, and the rest is history."

And pretty damn good history, too.

Canellis continues his role at FOX 32, which includes a Sunday night show entitled *The Sports Zone*. I've made several appearances on the show and enjoy it immensely. Canellis also remains the host of five TV shows the Bears produce—this while becoming a father, and a very happy one, at the age of 54. Daughter Gia is five.

Did I say, what more does Lou Canellis need?

# IN A CLASS BY THEMSELVES

# Bob Costas

AS IF this man needs an introduction. Bob Costas has been entrenched in the American sports consciousness for well over 40 years. He's been one of its leading voices, whether hosting a dozen Olympic games, calling Major League Baseball, or taking stands on controversial issues via programs such as *Costas Coast to Coast* and *On the Record with Bob Costas*. His remarkable run with NBC also included being the host and lead play-by-play announcer for the NBA, hosting 18 Kentucky Derbies, and being a major contributor to NFL broadcasts, a league he has harshly criticized. An iconic figure in the broadcast industry, it would be hard to chronicle all of Costas's achievements. Suffice it to say that there are many, but he also served as the Chicago Bulls play-by-play announcer during the 1979–80 season, albeit for only 19 road games. Costas made sure to point out that the Bulls went 2–17 during his broadcasts. There would be much better days ahead for both the Bulls and Costas, as NBC hired him soon after his short run with the team.

Costas has interviewed countless major figures, and not just in the world of sports. While hosting *Later* on NBC, Costas interviewed such famous guests as Paul McCartney, Martin Scorsese, Hank Aaron, and David Letterman.

Costas left NBC in 2019 but remains quite active, calling occasional baseball games for the MLB Network, appearing as a commentator for CNN, returning to HBO for *Back on the Record with Bob Costas*, and appearing on countless shows and podcasts such as this one. I told him he's become America's guest!

I first came into contact with Bob in 1975 during a college basketball game in St. Louis pitting Southern Illinois University and the University of Missouri. I was with SIU's head coach at the time, Paul Lambert, and Bob was with Jack Buck, the iconic voice of the

204 TELL ME A STORY I DON'T KNOW

*Bob Costas covering the Bulls for WGN Sports in 1979*

St. Louis Cardinals. He introduced Bob to us as his protégé. Little did we know then how Costas's career would skyrocket.

In 1980, Bob did a weekly radio show for the *Sporting News*, and I was one of his contributors. Those were the days when I was a full-time freelance journalist, so every gig I got earned me another dollar. The show could be heard nationally, but those of us who were contributors would receive a weekly album of the show. That's right, an album! The Internet hadn't been developed yet, and cell-phones were still a few years away. After that I would run into Bob when he would come to town for various broadcasts, and there were many. Did you know his first Super Bowl hosting assignment was in 1986 when the Bears trounced the New England Patriots? Two years before that, Bob did the play-by-play for one of the most memorable games in Wrigley Field history. It was the *NBC Game of the Week*, and it would be dubbed "the Sandberg Game" after the Cubs second baseman hit game-tying homers in the bottom of the ninth and 10th innings against the Cardinals' premier closer and future Hall of Famer Bruce Sutter. Bob also was part of the NBC broadcast crew that covered the Bulls' six NBA title runs, and he was behind the microphone for the last one in 1998, after a celebrated and tawdry incident got Marv Albert fired by the network. Bob called Michael Jordan's last shot with the Bulls, a championship game-winner against the Utah Jazz.

When I first approached Bob about doing my podcast, he said yes and was enthusiastic about it. As fluent, articulate, and exuberant as Bob is as an interviewer, he was that and then some being interviewed. He immediately goes into performance mode. What was most gratifying was after the podcast was dropped in February 2021, Bob sent me an email. Having been let go by WBBM Newsradio in July 2020, Bob said, "You will be back. You already are," adding, "You've got something special, great job, and glad to be one your guests." That gesture only made my journey into podcasting that much more rewarding.

Going back to that incredible game at Wrigley Field in 1984, Costas called it one of the most memorable games in baseball history.

"One of the important elements was it was the game of the week. You didn't have the proliferation of games on television that you do now. This had the attention of a huge portion of the baseball public. Many players who were going to play that night—that game had center stage. And then there was the setting: it's Wrigley Field, and it's the Cardinals—a friendly rivalry and not a bitter one like the Red Sox-Yankees or Dodgers-Giants."

It was a beautiful sun-kissed day on the North Side of Chicago, and Wrigley Field was decked out in in Cubbie blue, though there was a significant showing of Cardinals red in the stands.

"So now we get to the bottom of the 10th inning. Sandberg has tied the game with the first of his two homers off Sutter—it was 9-9. Willie McGee, who is almost a footnote to the game and hit for the cycle, delivers an RBI double [in the top of the 10th] and scores what looks to be an insurance run, so now the score is 11-9."

The Cubs looked finished. There were two out and nobody on.

"Bob Dernier gets a walk on a 3-2 pitch, and here comes Sandberg again. But here's the story you don't know, George. Some Chicago fans said through the years that I gave up on the Cubs because I started to read the credits."

This was standard, especially since there was there was another event scheduled, only in this case, delayed.

"There was a fight on *Sports World*. Marv Albert and Ferdie Pacheco [then known as "the Fight Doctor"] were standing by in Panama perhaps under the watchful eye of General Noriega. [Costas chuckles at his own sarcastic line.] They were literally holding the opening bell. The fighters were in the locker room for some 45 minutes because they weren't going to start the fight until the game was over!"

So now, as Costas explained, NBC was going to go to a hot switch when the game was over. In other words, a very quick transition.

"So I had to read the sponsors and the player of the game quickly. And then Sandberg homers to tie the game. We gave Sandberg complete credit. *The Natural* with Robert Redford had just come out, and I said something like, 'This may be the real-life Roy Hobbs!'"

That game propelled Sandberg to be a candidate for the MVP award, which he ended up winning. And the Cubs made the postseason for the first time since 1945. It's the signature game of his Hall of Fame career. The game had ended, but not for Costas, who ran into the Cubs' boisterous general manager, Dallas Green.

"Dallas Green, who I like very much and had done a great job during that time and making them a contender, came storming into the press room after the Cubs won the game in the 11th on a pinch hit by Dave Owen. Green yelled, "They all gave up on us! Costas gave up on us. NBC gave up on us."

At this point I'm howling with laughter at Costas's almost hysterical delivery.

"'And we came back, and he won it!'" he mimicked Green. "He had that John Wayne voice that could be heard in different area codes."

I interjected that Green was very intimidating, to which Costas chuckled and replied, "Yeah, he was a big man, he was very intimidating, but I liked him a lot. I understood the emotion of the moment, and I took it all as a positive, but that's a true story."

Here's another true story and yet another hallmark moment in Costas's career.

It was Game 6 of the 1998 NBA Finals in Utah between the then five-time champion Chicago Bulls and host Jazz. Costas had been thrust into the role of play-by-play voice, as opposed to hosting. That's because NBC had fired Marv Albert after the longtime voice of the NBA pled guilty to misdemeanor assault charges in a bizarre case involving cross-dressing and biting a woman in a hotel room. These finals were then documented along with the entire season as part of ESPN's wildly popular 10-part series, *The Last Dance*.

"Most of the era of the NBA on NBC from the early '90s through 2002 I hosted, but there were three seasons in which I did the play-by-play, and that was the first of three, and I fell into one of the memorable sports stories in American history."

But it was that final game and Michael Jordan's last shot that are indelibly etched in the memory of many sports fans.

"I think it's part of the play-by-play guy's job to be mindful of that and capture it in some way."

Costas was flanked by Doug Collins and Isiah Thomas, whose job it was to analyze the game action.

"There was no way to know how incredible that final sequence would be for Michael. He made the two free throws, then made a driving layup, then stole the ball from Karl Malone. He brought the ball up the court himself. No one else touches it, and then made the winning shot, holding the pose. It was a movie, and you had 10 takes. You couldn't get it any better. It was as if he was posing for a statue. What could be any better than that?"

I covered the home games, so naturally I was watching with friends, and yes, what could be better than that?

"On the other hand, the lead is 1 [87–86], and the Jazz have the ball with 5.2 seconds left. If they score, they force a Game 7. I thought I had to be mindful in that moment of that story, so I said something like, 'Who knows what will unfold in the next several weeks, but that may have been Michael Jordan's final shot in the NBA, and if that's the last image of Michael Jordan, how magnificent is it?'"

It wasn't, of course. But it was his last shot as a member of the Chicago Bulls. He would come out of retirement and sign as a free agent with the Washington Wizards in 2001.

"We knew all season long it was possible, maybe likely, this was the last go-around. And what I hadn't remembered until I watched *The Last Dance* was, before Game 5 with the Bulls leading three games to one in Chicago, I came on the air saying, 'If this is the last dance, it might as well be on their dance floor.' But they went back to the Delta Center for the Game 6 drama."

There were so many more dramatic moments in the illustrious career of Bob Costas, but we're proud some of them happened right here in Chicago.

# Michael Wilbon

I CAN'T think of anyone better to have debuted my podcast with. A kid from the South Side of Chicago who grew up a Cubs fan. Anomaly? Maybe. Abnormal? Sox fans might think so. His climb to journalistic fame and fortune began at Northwestern University. He was an award-winning sportswriter for the *Washington Post*, covering Major League Baseball, the NFL, and NBA before being promoted to columnist in 1990. Wilbon also covered 10 Olympic games and countless Super Bowls. But then, in 2001, he joined fellow sportswriter Tony Kornheiser on a path that would lead them to phenomenal success. ESPN's *Pardon the Interruption* continues to be appointment viewing and has garnered three Emmy Awards for outstanding daily studio show. It paired these longtime associates and friends who argue the topics of the day. The format is similar to that pioneered by film critics Roger Ebert and Gene Siskel, who competed against one another at different newspapers (the *Chicago Tribune* and *Chicago Sun-Times*) and joined forces in 1975 for the WTTW-TV series *Sneak Previews*, which they later took into syndication under various titles, their partnership lasting until Siskel's death in 1999.

Wilbon is affable, outspoken, argumentative, engaging, defiant, and as knowledgeable a sports journalist as you will find. He's not shy when it comes to offering an opinion or two on Twitter, especially when it comes to something related to Chicago sports! Catch him on a given Sunday, and he could be skewering the Bears. And he's blistered former White Sox manager Tony La Russa, too. Wilbon is also prominent on ESPN's telecasts of the NBA, and in 2020 was named to the National Sports Media Association Hall of Fame. He is also a Medill School of Journalism professor and trustee at Northwestern University.

I first met Wilbon sometime in the mid 1980s when he was in town covering one of the local teams. His amiable personality made it so easy to like him, having already respected his work in the *Washington Post*. His trips to town were numerous since the Bears were a premier team in the mid-1980s to early 1990s. Of course, there was also Michael Jordan and the Bulls, which brought Wilbon here so often he bought a home near downtown. Every time I saw Wilbon, he'd have a smile on his face, shake my hand, and the conversation flowed. It was as if we had known each other since childhood. I kind of wish we had. His rabid devotion to Chicago, its sports teams, and in particular, Northwestern is unrelenting.

During the Final Four of the 1990 NCAA Men's Basketball Tournament in Denver, I interviewed Wilbon and longtime journalist and Chicago sports radio talk show host Terry Boers about one aspect of the tournament. It was going to air on National Public Radio's *Morning Edition* the day after the championship game. But the piece was scrapped because on the eve of that championship game, CBS fired longtime host Brent Musburger, who had been the flagship announcer for the network. There went $240 in income!

When I first contacted Michael about being my first guest on *Tell Me a Story I Don't Know*, he didn't waver a minute. His enthusiasm allayed any fears I had about doing this in the first place. We found the right time in October 2020, and the interview was done on Zoom audio from his Maryland home. He was chock full of revealing stories from his childhood and of nearly returning to Chicago thanks to some pressure from the man I have dubbed the best sportswriter in the city's history.

"Around 1997 the great Bob Verdi [a title he so richly deserves], then columnist for the *Chicago Tribune* and probably my favorite sports columnist of my lifetime, decided it was time to leave the paper and do something else." Verdi would leave the *Tribune* for *Golf World* magazine—I delivered this news on 670 The Score when I worked there in such a somber manner, it was as if someone had died. I considered Verdi the best writer I ever read. That opinion hasn't changed.

*Ofman with Wilbon during the 2016 National League Championship Series*

"He said to me, 'It's time to come home. You're the person who should succeed me,'" said a surprised Wilbon. "It immediately freaked me out. The *Tribune* then started talking to me about coming home."

The pressure started to build for Wilbon, who admitted something I didn't know.

"I always wanted to work for the *Tribune* or *Sun-Times*. I delivered them—92 houses on Yale and Wentworth [on Chicago's South Side]. I had a paper route when I was 11 years old," Wilbon said gleefully. "I had the paper route until I went to Northwestern."

The *Tribune* began recruiting Wilbon, and during that period he received several phone calls, including one from Jay Mariotti, the tempestuous and controversial columnists for the *Sun-Times*. "Jay could foresee something I couldn't," Wilbon recalled,"and he was right. He could see sportswriters on TV. He always thought [it could be] the next Siskel and Ebert. There was no question Mariotti was clairvoyant."

In the end, Wilbon didn't come home. He resisted a chance to return to his Chicago roots, instead opting to stay at the *Washington Post*, proclaiming that it's the best job he could possibly have. "It was the hardest decision of my life not to come home."

It was around that time that Wilbon, his competing columnist at the *Post*, Tony Kornheiser, and others were part of picking the top athletes for ESPN's wonderful and award-winning series *SportsCentury*. They would be arguing from their offices about who should make the list. "Mark Shapiro was the executive producer of *SportsCentury*, and he would come to town and listen to me and Tony scream at one another across the hall. Shapiro remarked, he was going to put this on television."

Fast forward to 2001.

"Shapiro flies out to L.A., where I'm covering the NBA Finals. He has a new title, and as his first act, he wants to put me and Tony on television. That's your first act in this position? Your second act is you're going to get your ass fired! And he said, 'No, I'm going to do this, and if you two guys say no, I'm going to put someone else on.'"

You can just imagine what was going through Wilbon's head at this moment.

"We told Shapiro we don't want to be on something like *Crossfire*, which was on CNN. We wanted to be like Siskel and Ebert. The meeting lasted four hours! After I gathered my thoughts and sat in my car, I called Tony. It was 1:00 AM local time. It was 4:00 AM in the east, so I called Tony because I knew he would be walking his dog."

What followed was Wilbon telling Kornheiser why their lives were going to change. Both of them knew they could do what was being asked of them. And thus began *Pardon the Interruption,* one of the most celebrated sports shows, now in its 23rd year.

What I loved so much about the interview was Wilbon's unbridled enthusiasm. He was graphic in his descriptions and joyful to the point I just wanted the interview to keep going. He spoke from his heart, and anyone who knows Wilbon knows he has a very big heart. But we had time constraints. A good podcast, I was told, shouldn't go longer than 45 minutes. Since this one was going to be my first, I adhered to the formula. It actually ran 46 minutes, including the open, close, and commercial endorsements. I made sure newspaper writers who specialized in media coverage knew about the podcast, as did several TV shows. And having Wilbon was a boost.

Perhaps the very best part of this captivating conversation with Michael Wilbon was at the end, and it got me to thinking I might have something good on my hands. He blurted out, "It's cathartic! It's like being on the psychiatrist's sofa for an hour. I don't know if I should send you a check or you send me the bill!"

I sent him a thousand thank you's.

# Mike Greenberg

HE'S "GREENY," and everyone in the sports world knows that. As a matter of fact, there are probably many who don't follow sports very closely and still recognize the nickname. Mike Greenberg has become one this country's most famous and astute sports journalists, rising from an aspiring intern to the host of his own TV and radio show on ESPN. He reportedly earns in excess of $6.5 million annually and has also authored over a half dozen books. A graduate of Northwestern University, this native of New York began his career in Chicago, where he quickly established himself as a premier reporter for WSCR The Score. His prominence rose dramatically, with his coverage of Michael Jordan's attempt to play baseball to his reporting of the World Cup. But his appearance as a host of a local sports TV show led ESPN officials to hire him in 1996. By 2000 he was cohosting a national radio show on the network with Mike Golic called *Mike and Mike*. The extremely popular collaboration lasted some 18 years before the network hired Greenberg to anchor *Get Up* in 2018, a morning TV sports program that has been on ever since. Greenberg also added duties as the network's *NBA Countdown* studio host. A gregarious figure with movie star looks, Greenberg has been compared to Bob Costas for his ability to cleanly and concisely articulate opinions and thoughts while commanding panel guests.

Three of Greenberg's books—*All You Could Ask For; Why My Wife Thinks I'm an Idiot: The Life and Times of a Sportscaster Dad;* and *Mike and Mike's Rules for Sports and Life*—were all on the *New York Times* bestseller list, and his latest is *Got Your Number: The Greatest Sports Legends and the Numbers They Own.*

Now in his mid-fifties, Greenberg is truly enjoying life at the top. His son attends Northwestern, and his daughter is a recent

*The author (about 25 years ago), not Groucho Marx*

graduate. I'm very proud to call Greeny a friend. Just consider the foreword he wrote for the book. But seriously, I look nothing like Groucho. Actually, there are times I sound more like Harpo!

I was flabbergasted and humbled by Greeny's recollection and the way he wrote it in the foreword. I'm forever grateful. But there's a story behind this story.

I had been trying to get hold of Greeny for months. I texted and called him several times and no return. Very odd. Then I decided to go through his wife Stacy's Twitter account. Well, she hadn't seen it, and a month later gave me Greeny's cell—only it was different from the one I had. Greeny explained he changed it a year ago but failed to mention it to a number of people. We had a wonderful conversation, and he said he would gladly write the foreword, which he did that day!

As for the person I texted and called? Who knows?

Greeny and I were actually hired by the Score on the same day, December 28, 1991, which happens to be my birthday. The Score debuted on January 2, 1992. Greeny was a joy to work and socialize with. He not only had talent but a personality to match, and it was very easy to tell he was headed for success. Greeny exclaimed he wanted to be an actor, but he couldn't act, sing, or dance. What he could do very well was observe. It was a skill he honed in his early days of broadcasting.

And, oh, did I mention he danced at my wedding and I, at his?

Greeny is a great storyteller—witness the many books he's written. He's sharp, quick-witted, and well-versed on any topic. As baseball spring training approached in 1994, we had already learned Michael Jordan was going to camp with the Chicago White Sox. I was sent to Mesa, Arizona, to cover the Cubs, and Greeny was sent to Sarasota, Florida, to cover the White Sox, which would turn out to be a surreal adventure, to say the least.

"That was one of the best experiences I ever had, following Michael around," Greeny recalled. "The day we get down there, his first day, there must have been 200 reporters. Ted Koppel hosted *Nightline* from the ballpark. The ballpark was jam-packed with reporters, mobbed! Within two or three days, there was just the *Chicago Sun-Times, Tribune, Daily Herald*, and me."

It was then Greeny went from being a reporter to describing his living conditions.

"The three baseball reporters had the budget to stay in the hotel. There was only one hotel in Sarasota those days, and it was the Ritz-Carlton. The Score didn't have the budget, and I was there for six weeks! So we rented a room on Siesta Key in a six-bedroom house. I just had a room."

This is where the story takes a comical turn in a way only Greeny can describe.

"The other five occupants of this house were women. I would say the median age was eighty-seven!"

This drew sustained laughter from the two of us.

"You remember what our job was...we had to call in and do live reports on the radio, and there were no cellphones."

Actually, I had one in Mesa, but back then it was one of those brick phones about the size of a...well, a brick.

"I would pick up the phone, which was just one line everybody would use, and there were times when I was on the air and one of the women would start dialing! There was a pay phone across the street, so I would do my updates from there."

Back before technology made our jobs easier, we had equipment we needed for transmitting tape-recorded audio clips over the phone. Remember the telephone? We would unscrew the receiver portion and attach what were called alligator clips to it and the corresponding outlet on our tape recorders. Then we would plug our microphones into the recorder and be able to talk and transmit sound at the same time. This was an issue for Greeny, because you couldn't unscrew a pay phone. He forged ahead just the same.

"I had to make those calls from the pay phone because the women were ruining my reports. The women didn't understand what was happening. They don't understand I'm on the radio, and what does that really mean to them?"

But this wasn't Greeny's favorite story about covering Jordan in spring training. It was about Jordan's rather dubious debut. "If you might recall, Jordan went 0 for his first 18 or something like that [actually 0-for-14], and it was very embarrassing, and he was quite upset by it. There was a lot of criticism of him. *Sports Illustrated* had a cover that said Michael Jordan and the White Sox are embarrassing baseball. There was a lot of negative stuff going on."

Remember, there were only four reporters covering the Sox after the first few days of his baseball career, and Greeny was one of them.

"The White Sox were on the road in some small town [Fort Myers, Florida], and it was a rainy night. There couldn't have been more than 300 people in the stands. Jordan comes up and he swings out of his shoes! He gets fooled on a fastball but manages to top it into the ground, a little dribbler down the third-base line, and he beats it out for a base hit."

After the game, Greeny and the other three reporters go down to interview Jordan.

"It was a tiny little clubhouse, smaller than the locker room in my high school. And they were dumping beer on him—and those were good White Sox teams. There was Frank Thomas, Jack McDowell,

Robin Ventura, and Alex Fernandez. Jordan is stripped to the waist and they're giving him a beer shower. When that was done, we go over and ask him a few questions. He was happy he got his first hit. And when we were walking out, something moved me to turn around and look at him. It's a vision I'll never forget. He's sitting on a bench in this tiny little locker room with a cigar, stripped to the waste and covered with cheap beer, and he had a smile, a look of satisfaction on his face that rivaled anything I'd ever seen before."

Greeny had already covered some of the NBA titles Jordan and the Bulls had won. What Greeny amplified was, "In life, you have to celebrate the little dribblers because life has more of those than grand slam home runs. But I knew then he would go back to basketball. I didn't know when, but I knew he would."

It's safe to say that Mike Greenberg has hit more grand slams in his professional and personal life than dribblers.

# Alan Schwartz

ALAN SCHWARTZ was one of the great movers and shakers in the world of tennis. Back in 1969 he, along with his father, built the Midtown Tennis Club (now Midtown Athletic Club) in Chicago, then the largest indoor tennis facility in the U.S., only recently surpassed. He once served as vice president and then president of the United States Tennis Association (USTA) and coined its mission statement: "To promote and develop the growth of tennis." That he did, and then some. Alan was a gifted player at Yale, an astute businessman, and one of the most thoughtful and giving human beings you would ever want to meet. I say *was*, and with great sadness. Alan died on December 2, 2022, at the age of 91. What shocked and saddened me even further was we had our semiannual lunch just three days earlier! He was as vibrant as ever, telling me new stories with great panache. I couldn't wait to start discussing the upcoming Australian Open with him.

What I want to convey to you is how important this gentleman was, not only to tennis, but to his family, his associates, and yours truly. His passion for humanity was inspiring.

Two stories of note I want to share with you. First, how Alan and his dad managed to build the Midtown Tennis Club despite enormous adversity and how it was aimed at women.

"We were turned down by literally 16 Chicago banks," he told me. "They said it was too risky and what if tennis doesn't work? We were prepared with a warehouse and other things, but they didn't want to take a chance. Then my wife spotted an article in the paper about this disliked banker in Detroit who was breaking away and paying people more interest than anyone else in town. She said, 'Wasn't this your friend Don from school?' I said yes, and she said, 'Why don't you call him?'"

*Alan Schwartz with the author*

Being the entrepreneurial businessman he was, Schwartz made the trip to Detroit the next day.

"I told him my story. I was well prepared with architect drawings and the projections galore. All kinds of possibilities—why it would work and the market was out there. And he said, 'Oh, it's been a pleasure talking to you. You got the mortgage, don't worry about that.' I said, 'Well, I've got the architects' drawings and projections. Don't you want to see those?' And he said, 'No, it'll be a very pretty building, no doubt. And you lose a little money in your first year, and your projection broke even in the second and made money in the third year, and good forever after.'"

It stood to reason what Schwartz asked next. Why did his banker friend in Detroit say yes to the loan while 16 bankers in Chicago said no?

"He said, 'Two reasons: You were one of the guys on the varsity willing to play down and practice with me, even though I would never get up to the varsity level, and I appreciated that. And second, you would kill yourself before you give up on a point, and you'll do the same thing making this successful. I'll take my chances.'"

Now you're getting an idea what kind of determined and kind human being Schwartz was.

But Midtown wasn't going to be a bastion for men and their rackets. No. Schwartz, being the savvy businessman, realized in order to make Midtown successful, he needed to involve women. Otherwise, he would be doomed.

"And so the challenge was, how do you get women more actively involved? And I'm not sure that story has been told as much as it should have been told, as important as it was. The first thing we did was to develop what turned out to be the only patented tennis program the U.S. had authorized. It was designed just for women, and it was called Tennis in No Time."

I remember that, and some of the smartly crafted ads in the newspaper that had a huge impact.

"The ads, as corny as they were—the original ads for TNT [Tennis in No Time] was a coy picture of the *Mona Lisa* with a tennis racket superimposed in her hand, so there'd be no question the fact that this was a tennis ad. And we were bolstered at that time in the change in the advertising world that began to show tennis as part of the sophisticated ad, whether it was for Cadillac or scotch, and then tennis clothes for women became fashionable. That gave us the spark to separate ourselves from any of the competition."

If you watch tennis now or even in the last number of years, some sponsors include such high-end companies as Rolex and Mercedes-Benz, to name a few.

"Without question, women actually made the difference, because you're open 18 hours a day, but of those hours, 9:00 to 5:00

are hours you basically have to be dependent on women, except for a few retired men, perhaps. You had to fill those hours, and women were the logical ones.

"There was actually a point in time when the women [tennis] pros were better known than the men, or any other sports. What sport was there where you could rattle off six first names?"

Well, there was Chris (Evert), Billie Jean (King), Martina (Navratilova), Virginia (Wade), Rosie (Casals), and a little later on Anna (Kournikova).

"They became famous, and it starts with just first names. That's pretty important."

Several years ago, Schwartz allowed his family to take Midtown Tennis Club down a new path, the transformation into an athletic club. That meant a significant rehab, including a hotel, swimming pools, gyms, restaurants, and a bevy of other new facilities. The project cost an estimated $85 million and just a year after completion, COVID hit—and with it, a big hit to Midtown's other facilities scattered in different parts of the country and Montreal. Most have recovered, but not all at 100 percent.

Finally, I want to relay this poignant yet still hard for me to believe story of how Alan and I met. I was doing a Saturday afternoon talk show on 670 The Score. It was mid-March 2002, and I was declaring my love for the NCAA basketball tournament, and the fact that I had covered four Final Fours. But I also mentioned my love for and great desire to attend my favorite event, the U.S. Open Tennis Tournament. I had never been and vowed one day, I would finally go. So, after the show, I went to listen to my voicemails and heard this deep voice declare, "Hello, George, this is Alan Schwartz, and I'm the vice president of the USTA, and I really enjoyed hearing your desire to attend a U.S. Open. So I'm inviting you and a friend to be my guest in the President's Box for the upcoming Open."

I started screaming into the phone. "*Who are you?...and, Yes!*" I was in total disbelief. Alan gave me the name and number of his secretary, so of course, first thing Monday morning, I called to confirm this surreal call. "Yes," Juanita, his secretary, said on the other end. "Alan has invited you and a friend to the 2002 Open. I will send you the invitations." Two days later, reality. There they were, invites to Friday in the President's Box and two tickets for anywhere on the grounds Saturday. I called my dear friend from high school Andy Bloom, who was also an avid tennis player, and he said he would love to go. And we did. Lucky for us, though the event was rained out Thursday and Sunday, it was not the two days we were there. Alan greeted us and took us on a tour of the grounds. I was still wondering to myself, *Who is this incredibly generous person who is spending over a half an hour wandering about this famous complex?* Then we took our seats in the President's Box, where we were handed glasses of champagne and introduced to the presidents of Wimbledon and the French Open. Then we watched Serena Williams and Pete Sampras dispatch their opponents with ease.

I will never forget that weekend or the incredible kindness Alan showed me then and in subsequent years.

I'm still so sad he's gone now, but he will forever be my tennis angel.

# Mark Giangreco

HE'S ONE of the great characters in our business, or was. Mark Giangreco was fired in March 2021 from his longtime role as lead sports anchor at WLS-TV, the ABC affiliate in Chicago, for a remark he made about a fellow news anchor Cheryl Burton. It wasn't the first time Giangreco was in hot water with the station, but this was the last straw. The immensely popular and irreverent Giangreco said Burton was someone who could play the ditzy, combative interior decorator on some made up show. She complained to management, which decided it had had enough. Gone then, was one of the city's most creative and diligent journalists, who made watching TV sports here a unique experience. Giangreco was the top earning sports anchor in town, although his salary had been recently cut. During his run, Giangreco was earning seven figures. The Buffalo, New York, native was hired by Channel 5, the NBC affiliate in Chicago, in 1982, and it didn't take long for him to establish his brand in what was then a cutthroat market. He spent 12 years there before being lured by ABC 7. Giangreco's gimmicks earned him quite a reputation, along with three suspensions.

Giangreco's creativity included an occasional segment called, "Make Mark Do Your Job," in which he would do things such as being a kindergarten teacher. It drew rave reviews. Giangreco also hosted a New Year's Eve show with fellow station reporter Janet Davies, which was a ratings bonanza for the station.

I knew when I first met Mark in 1982, while covering a baseball meeting at one of the O'Hare hotels, that he was different. He dressed in a white trenchcoat, and while he was just getting his feet wet in a new city, there was an air of confidence surrounding this guy. The more I watched him, the more I appreciated what he was trying to do. But more importantly, the more I watched him work, the more I understood what a first-class reporter and journalist he was. It didn't take Mark long to compile a cadre of sources. He could break stories with the best of them, but his entertainment value was off the charts. Take all of those traits and wrap them into a quality human being with three grown sons now, all of whom played hockey, Mark's first and true love.

Mark told me stories galore, but by far, the most entertaining involved former Chicago Bear star Steve McMichael who, as of June 2023, is battling ALS. McMichael was hired by the NBC affiliate as a Sunday night contributor during the Bears' season. Little did they realize, though perhaps they should have, the havoc he and Giangreco would create.

"We're talking about the culture of the '80s and '90s," Giangreco recalled, "when you can say or do things that were so bizarre and get away with them. The primary battleground for sports back then were those Bears Sunday night shows. Channel 7 had Walter Payton; Channel 2 had Mike Ditka, head coach of the team; and we at Channel 5 had Steve 'Mongo' McMichael, who was the scariest, craziest guy I ever met. But a lot of people don't realize he's also one of the smartest, really introspective guys I've ever met."

McMichael was a standout defensive tackle during the Bears' formative and great teams during the 1980s. He played on their Super Bowl championship team of 1985 and was considered one of the linchpins to their dynamic defense. He was also one of the many characters on the Bears roster, hence a reason Giangreco and Channel 5 took the gamble of hiring him for the Sunday night shows.

"Those Sunday night shows were so outrageous. Back then, he would bring props. He would think things out, and after every Bears game, he would go out and get absolutely hammered. And he'd stumble down to the studio with his entourage—his wife, his mother in-law, who had a filthier mouth than he did, smoking butts and had a beer in her hands. And they'd bring all their friends, and McMichael would call her friends the Kotex mafia!"

If you didn't know who McMichael was, you're probably creating a visual picture of what this might have looked like. Bizarre would appropriate but perhaps even an understatement.

"They would sit there, and Mongo had his props. One night he brought in a giant hypodermic needle, and he said, "You know, I've been hanging out with you pretty closely. I'm going to have to give you an AIDS test, and he sticks it in my neck! And, ha, ha, ha, that was so outrageous."

What McMichael didn't know was that an AIDS story was the lead in that evening's newscast. A woman had died from contracting it from her dentist.

"So that was it! They fired him! And the general manager, if we back up a few years, came to me and said, 'Why don't we hire McMichael? He seems pretty crazy, and you can just control him.' Well, I wasn't about to control him. I just cut him loose. If you want the gorilla in the room, here you go."

The two did all kinds of bits, from McMichael bringing in his little dog Pepe on the set with a spiked collar. He hit Giangreco with a pie, cut off his tie, and got him in a headlock that almost rendered him unconscious. There was more.

"I remember when the airplane phone was a big technological advance, and they would be playing a West Coast game, and he'd do the show on the phone from the charter plane. I drew a cartoon with his head sticking out of the plane, and he said, 'You better not be showing a picture of me with my head sticking out of the plane.' And I said we would never do that, and on and on we went. He would bring on other players who would beat me up. He would light things on fire."

In other words, McMichael was one dangerous dude.

"The night they fired him for that comment, he went into the lobby of the brand new NBC Tower with all these huge murals of famous NBC broadcasters [I worked there for a time and remember how splendid it looked]. He tore down every picture and smashed everything in the lobby. He had a can of spray paint, which he would bring all the time, and they had this beautiful etched logo of the peacock in a huge glass entranceway. He sprayed genitals on the peacock."

Yes, those were the very wild days of television, but Giangreco also recalled a much tamer version of McMichael.

"I remember taking my kids to Halas Hall, where the Bears trained, and he came up to me and said, 'Are these your kids?' I said, 'Yeah,' and he said, 'I didn't know you were married.'"

His two eldest boys were about eight and six at the time.

"My youngest one was too small to make the trip. He takes them into the locker room, gives them footballs, autograph jerseys, sweatbands. And here's Richard Dent and a bunch of the other guys smoking cigars and playing cards naked! He was such a kind, introspective guy. We became great friends. He was one of the smartest guys I ever knew."

Before the season, the Bears held training camp in Platteville, Wisconsin, where the McMichael hijinks were always present.

"I would be talking to his wife, Debra, who would show up in a bikini, sometimes in spandex. And she would drive her bike up to me during my live shot. And during calisthenics, he would turn and say, 'I see you with my wife, I'm gonna kick your ass.' It would go on and on like that. It was must-see television."

People would first turn on Channel 5 to see what Giangreco and McMichael were up to and then turn to Channel 2 to watch Ditka. This is where Giangreco derived great pleasure.

"I would make fun of Ditka on every single show. The guy's a football coach. He's not the pope. He's not a president, he's not a king. I couldn't believe how people worshiped him. I remember one night we brought a TV monitor on the set to watch CBS, which was what no one back then would think of doing. And Mongo and I would make fun of Ditka. Those are the kind of things we did. It was renegade, wild west TV."

It was, and I watched it every Sunday night. Today, it's homogenized, but back then it was appointment viewing. I don't think we'll ever see that again unless, maybe, YouTube?

# Wayne Messmer

HE'S THE voice of Chicago...and the nation! Wayne Messmer's baritone has been heard booming the national anthem and "God Bless America" at stadium venues all over Chicago for nearly 40 years. But this accomplished musician also performs locally, singing beautiful standards that draw many avid and loyal fans. Messmer is also a radio host, professional speaker, author, part owner of the Chicago Wolves minor league hockey team, and co-owner of Wayne Messmer & Associates LLC, a financial services firm.

But it's his rendition of the anthem Messmer is best known for, and it all began when he became the PA announcer for the Loyola University hockey team. He determined a taped version of the anthem before the game didn't cut it, so he volunteered to sing it. His rendition was so good, the players were banging their sticks in approval. His first gig professionally was with the then Chicago Sting pro soccer team. That exposure led him to the Blackhawks for 13 years. But during that time, Messmer also handled the task for the White Sox for three years. Immediately after that, in 1985, Messmer joined the Cubs, and when the Wolves got started in 1994, he performed for them. He's been with the Cubs and Wolves ever since. Messmer will occasionally be joined by his wife, an accomplished singer and actor.

Wayne has been singing the anthem about as long as I have been reporting games, meaning I've heard him sing at least a thousand times, and his rendition always sends chills up my spine. Every time I see him, I sing his name, only I'm not quite a baritone, nor do I carry a note as well as Wayne. He is as affable and funny a guy as you would want to meet. And that's the way he was during our interview. He darted quips often, but there are two stories I want to share where quips weren't needed.

The first involved a rendition of the anthem that introduced Wayne to a national audience and became a signature moment. The second was a traumatic experience that nearly cost him his life.

It was January 1991, and the NHL All-Star Game is being played at the Chicago Stadium. The old barn was filled to the rafters. Among the hometown Blackhawks represented in the game: Jeremy Roenick, Steve Larmer, and Chris Chelios. The crowd was jacked up, but for more than just their hometown heroes. It was also during the Gulf War, which became fuel for one of the most dramatic renditions ever sung.

"NBC was covering the game that year, and they had opted out of the anthem on a game played there earlier in the year," Messmer remembers. "The fans weren't happy about that. It was during the Gulf War, so the emotions were running high, and patriotism was in an enhanced state. We knew NBC was going to cover the Canadian and national anthems in their entirety, and if we have to break away for a new bulletin of any kind it's not going to happen!"

Messmer was very happy with that decision.

"It's rare what we are God-gifted to do and, requested by man, we meet at the same intersection. But that certainly was it. That was where, if you're ever going to do this thing right, this is it."

So, with Al Melgard at the mighty Stadium organ, he began playing the intro to the anthem, and there was a sudden burst of cheering from the crowd. It was as if someone had scored a goal. Then Messmer began belting out the anthem, and even the extremely noisy crowd couldn't drown him out. *O say can you see, by the dawn's early light...* The crowd got louder and louder, not only waving flags but lit sparklers, as well.

Messmer had a lot on his shoulders.

"It was so emotional that it took intense concentration, because it's tough to sing with a giant emotional lump in your throat when you're about to burst into tears." *And the rocket's red glare, the bombs bursting in air.*

The decibel level was indescribable. I was in the press box and considered plugging my ears.

*...and the home of the brave?*

Messmer had mastered an uptick to the word *brave* and a lasting vibrato that had become his trademark. The crowd was delirious.

"When I finished, I was like a wet dish rag. I sweated through both of the anthems. And Kathleen [Messmer's wife] was with me up in the organ loft, and I gave her a big hug and said, 'Ooh, we just did something.'"

That became very evident when the two arrived home.

"Every local and national newscast opened and closed with that video, and I said, 'Wow, this was quite a day.'"

When I suggested to Messmer that his might have been one of the most memorable renditions of the anthem ever sung in this country's history, he agreed.

"It is, and I happened to be the guy there, and I fortunately had the ability and gift at the time to do it right, and a time when we needed to hear it right. The game was broadcast to the troops through Armed Forces Radio, and some years later I'm singing at an event at Chicago's McCormick Place. So I'm backstage...and all of a sudden, this giant meat-hook of a hand comes down on my shoulder. And the person with this hand says, 'Wayne, thank you for singing *the* song the way it's supposed to be sung when we needed to hear it right.'"

Mesmer said, "You're welcome," and blurted out the name, "General Norman Schwarzkopf." And I said, "Wow!" Schwarzkopf was the commander of coalition forces during the Gulf War.

Then, about three and a half years after the pinnacle of his career at the NHL All-Star Game, in April 1994, Messmer's career, not to mention his life, was jeopardized.

"It was after a Blackhawks game on a Friday night. I was walking back to my car, which was a block and a half away. I almost got to my car, and I saw a young man walking down the street about four car lengths away, and I kept my eye on him as I got into my car. I started my car and began pulling out of the parking space and didn't realize this 16-year-old, who I had my eye on, just stood there as a 15-year-old ran up on me, and as I pulled out of this parking space he banged on the window. Bam, bam, and then [with a noise he made of a gunshot] pulls the trigger."

It was a 9 mm gun shot at point-blank range. The bullet shot through the glass and struck Messmer in the neck.

"At a moment like that, people talk about their life flashing before their eyes. I just thought, survival. I hit the gas and took off. Never saw the kid who pulled the trigger. Before I took off, I looked at the young man standing there and gave me a little bit of a start in the first place, and he's standing under a streetlamp."

Messmer was trying to get a closer look at the young man because he might be the only eyewitness to his attempted murder!

"I didn't know how bad I was hurt, which was fortunate. But I drove a block and a half back from where I came from [the old Chicago Stadium], parked the car, walked backed to where I was, knocked on the door, and, talk about a buzzkill...here's anthem boy bleeding like something out of the old west, and I couldn't make a sound. It was like a death gurgle."

At that point, Messmer sat down and waited for the ambulance to arrive.

"One person who sat by me was a nursing student and a friend, and I'll never forget that kindness. We went to County Hospital, where they did a 10-hour surgery. I woke up two and a half days later with a lot of questions. I had no voice and was on a respirator, I had IVs going every imaginable place. And they had done a tracheotomy so they could open my throat up from ear to ear."

It took a while for Messmer to become conscious again and begin to understand what had happened to him.

"Is this a nightmare? Well, yes. But did it really happen? Yes. And I have to maintain a sense of humor to keep from imploding. So I write down on a slate to Kathleen...I imagine myself looking like a Pez dispenser on the operating table. She said, 'You are as crazy as ever.' And then she said, 'We should try our best for a complete recovery.'"

The one thing Messmer was sure of was who he was, and he wasn't going to change. But he also realized what he had done for a living may have come to an end. Fortunately for Messmer and his fans, it didn't.

"Six months and five days later was the first ever Chicago Wolves home game at the Allstate Arena, then the Rosemont Horizon. I walked in and sang before 17,000 fans and felt like, 'I can walk on water!' It gave me a tremendous message that 'you're not done yet.'"

The number of things Messmer has done since are attributed to an understanding that there is still work to be done. And he's has been doing that, along with singing the anthem, and we are all grateful for that.

# Greg Gumbel

HIS LIST of achievements is endless. Greg Gumbel has been a guest in your living room, den, radio, phone, iPad, or wherever you watch or listen to sports for 50 years! Whether it was from a studio, a baseball, football, or basketball game, or an Olympic venue, Gumbel has presided over myriad major sporting events. But he's most synonymous with the NCAA men's basketball tournament, an event he's hosted for 26 years! It's one of, if not *the* premier event on the sports calendar, particularly the first round, which finds Gumbel and his studio analysts navigating coverage of 48 games over four days! Gumbel was also part of CBS's NFL broadcast team, partnering with analyst Adam Archuleta, until he stepped from football in March 2023.

Now in his second half-century in the industry, the outspoken Gumbel made history being the first African American to broadcast a Super Bowl (XXXV). He was the first morning show host for all-sports radio WFAN in New York. He also replaced Brent Musburger as the host of the very popular *NFL Today* on CBS. Gumbel has worked for ESPN, Madison Square Garden Network, NBC, and CBS.

You might also be familiar with Greg's brother, Bryant, a very accomplished and award-winning sports journalist who is currently the host of the long-running HBO series *Real Sports with Bryant Gumbel*. Both brothers got their starts in the early 1970s, Bryant in Los Angeles and Greg in Chicago, where he was the sports anchor for WMAQ-TV, the NBC affiliate.

I met Greg when I broke into the Chicago media in 1978. A friendly figure with a ferocious appetite to succeed, Greg and I would see each other at many sporting events. While the radio sports industry was just growing, TV sports had taken a foothold in the American consciousness. And local sportscasters became household names and very visible, since TV news ratings were rising.

Greg was ever so gracious in doing what turned out to be my first split two-part show. The first part began the week before the 2022 NFL season and the second, days before the 2023 NCAA Tournament. One thing is very evident: Greg is not shy about offering his opinion. Now 77, it sounds as if it doesn't really matter to him.

"I started in April of 1973. Johnny Morris was my boss. I was a sports reporter Wednesday, Thursday, and Friday, and on the air Saturday and Sunday. I was there for seven and a half years before leaving for ESPN. Both my brother and I don't ever hesitate to say how very fortunate we were to begin where we began. We were in local sports markets where sportscasters only dream of reaching."

But Gumbel believes he was in the right place at the right time. African Americans were rare in the TV sports business.

"I believe that is why I got hired at Channel 5 in Chicago, and that's why I got hired at ESPN—because there weren't very many, if any, Black faces on the air. Here I was, with no broadcast experience whatsoever. Now, that's not why you stay. You stay because you show them you can do the job. I don't believe that was why I was hired at the Garden in New York or at CBS."

Born in New Orleans, the Gumbel brothers grew up in the Hyde Park neighborhood of Chicago and had a joyous time as kids, already knowing what they wanted to be. They would grab their gloves and stand in front of a mirror and pretend they were announcers.

"Winding up and pitching and even describing the pitch," Gumbel declared with sarcastic glee. "And that's not the worst of it. My dear mom used to talk about how we had one of those hockey games where you slide the players back and forth."

Oh, do I remember that!

"We had all six uniforms from the Original Six in the NHL. We would divide the game up into three periods, and we would have one set of the players from the Chicago Blackhawks, and one set from the Montreal Canadiens, and we would keep goal scores and assists. Second period, you change the identities of those guys to their second lines and third period to their third lines. But the worst part was our mother would shake her head because we were doing play-by-play at the same time! And it wasn't a far stretch, she would wait for our father to come home so she could say, 'Wait until you see what these idiots did today.'"

Gumbel loved his time growing up in Chicago. The family first moved there after their father graduated from Georgetown University in Washington, D.C.

"Loved it. We lived in Hyde Park, a very liberal and racially diverse neighborhood. Lived right across the street from George Williams College on 53$^{rd}$ and Drexel. They had a big field out there, and Bryant I would play baseball and football from morning until night."

But the brothers differed when it came to their team allegiances for understandable reasons.

"I was a Chicago Cardinals football fan, and Bryant was the Bears fan. Why was I a Cardinals fan? Because I was a White Sox fan, and the Cardinals played at Comiskey Park. And Bryant was a Cubs fan because I was a White Sox fan, and because the Cubs played at Wrigley Field, which is where the Chicago Bears played."

Got that?

"So we're out in front of our building throwing the football around, and these guys come up and say, 'Hi, can we throw the football around with you?' We said sure. So we're throwing the football around back and forth, and our parents had gone grocery shopping. Twenty minutes later, they come back, and my dad walks over and starts talking to these guys. And they converse for a couple of minutes, and these guys say, 'Thanks for letting us throw the ball around with you,' and they left. My dad comes over and says, 'Ollie Matson and Night Train Lane.' We didn't know at the time, but they would become two future NFL Hall of Famers."

Little did they realize then how the Gumbel kids would really wind up. Now, here's a bit of an oddity: neither Gumbel brother ever took a course in broadcasting.

"I'm not a believer it's a necessity," he said. "I'm a believer it can help. You probably can learn a lot of technicalities that I would learn on the job. My brother and I have never shied away from saying our dad was easily the biggest influence in our lives. He had three things outlined, he repeated them constantly: 'Think clearly, listen carefully, and speak distinctively.' Those tenants will guide you well in the world of broadcasting. I think that [it's important that] you're able to think for yourself and...you're able to say what you think in a convincing manner, without talking down to your audience."

This got Gumbel going. And like I said, he's never been shy about offering his opinion.

"There are a lot of people in my business who talk down to their audience. It's kind of like the approach of, I know everything. Sit back and let me tell you what this is all about."

The conversation then led into sports radio, where Gumbel wouldn't hold back.

"I'm not a fan of sports talk radio because people who listen to sports talk radio strike me as being anxious to be told what to think. I certainly don't need someone yelling at me. I don't want anyone telling me what I should think about this pitcher, who I can watch for myself and make my own judgment. If you're tuning in to hear people argue and scream and shout, that's fine. Good luck to you, good luck to you in your early grave! I think it's the most ridiculous thing on the planet."

When I reminded Gumbel that he was the first morning drive anchor at all-sports WFAN in New York, he responded succinctly, "That's where I learned to hate it! It was something new and different, so I thought I would try it, and about three or four months into a three-year contract, I knew it wasn't for me because I didn't want to sit and argue, but that's what the audience wanted. What I tried to do was to get people to sit and talk with me about what that team was doing."

What Gumbel preferred was having announcers from area teams come on and talk about what their teams did the night before.

"In general, I didn't like it and didn't enjoy it. There have been a couple of situations where I've been in my career where I started something and I realized after I got into it that I wasn't going to continue it or go back to it."

A few publications picked up on our interview and proceeded to rip Gumbel for his views.

Like him or not, Gumbel has endured successfully for half a century and has done it his way. Can't argue with that.

# Acknowledgments

HILLARY CLINTON wrote a book titled *It Takes a Village*.

She was right.

Doing my podcast and then writing a book on it took many people to accomplish. And it wouldn't have happened without an inspiration. Several years ago, I was invited by WSCR host Laurence Holmes to be a guest on his podcast *House of L*. I thought it was going to be about what's happening in Chicago sports, but instead it was about me! I started talking about my career and growing up in Chicago. It was incredibly refreshing. I'm certain, whether consciously or subconsciously, this is why I did the podcast—interviewing sports personalities beyond the realm of their business. So thank you, Laurence.

Sam Ofman. He's one of my nephews and worked for Triumph Books while living in Chicago. He played a major role in hooking me up with the right people there and encouraged me. Love you, "AM."

And thank you T.J. Rives, the sideline reporter for the Tampa Bay Buccaneers. He's the man behind finding homes for my podcast and being ever the optimist. I'm not sure where I would be without him.

Thanks yous also go out to Will Hatczel, who does my mixing, and Nick Tocci, who picked up the graphic chores from Tatiana Shinkan. Lots of talent here.

And how can you do a podcast and subsequently write a book without the guests? Only 51 made this one, and I hope the rest make another. I can't thank them enough for providing riveting, emotional, and sometimes hilarious stories. It made my job a joy.

To the folks at Triumph Books: you took on a unique concept and let me run with it. I had a blast writing it.

Last and definitely not least, my wife, Elizabeth, who was thrilled I took on this challenge and encouraged me along the way. She's lived with a sports enthusiast for 35 years and understands how passionate I am about my business. Thank you, Gorgeous.

# About the Author

GEORGE OFMAN has spent a half-century in the sports broadcasting business. From his time as sports director at WSIU Radio and TV at Southern Illinois University to one of the originals at SportsPhone in the late 1970s to his current role as writer and producer of the *Tell Me a Story I Don't Know* podcast, George has carved out what he calls a very rewarding career. It included 20 years as a freelance journalist with clients including National Public Radio, the CBC in Canada, and the BBC in Great Britain. George was also an original member of WSCR The Score, Chicago's first all-sports station for 17 years and where he established the weekly baseball show *Hit and Run* in 2005. The show is still going strong. He also was an anchor/reporter on Chicago's all-news station WBBM-780 for 10 years. During his career, George has had the pleasure of covering the Super Bowl champion Bears, six Bulls titles, three Blackhawks Stanley Cup championships, and the end of two lengthy baseball droughts: the White Sox' World Series title in 2005 and the Cubs' in 2016. He's covered countless major events, including Pete Rose tying baseball's all-time hits record at Wrigley Field; Walter Payton's rushing record; the "Sandberg Game"; thoroughbred racing's Cigar capturing a record 16th straight victory at Arlington Park; numerous tennis tournaments with star players such as John McEnroe, Jimmy Connors, Chris Evert, and Martina Navratilova; and so much more. *Tell Me a Story I Don't Know* first aired on January 26, 2021.

George has won numerous awards for his work, including three from the Illinois Broadcasters Association.

George boasts, and rightfully so, that he's the only person to have witnessed the highest scoring game in NBA and NHL game in history! And yes, he covered the 23–22 game at Wrigley Field in 1979. A tennis enthusiast, George wishes his legs were 10 years younger but can still run the court.